✧ *Companions for the Journey* ✧

Praying with
Thomas Merton

✧ *Companions for the Journey* ✧

Praying with Thomas Merton

by
Wayne Simsic

Saint Mary's Press
Christian Brothers Publications
Winona, Minnesota

In gratitude
✧ *to my friend* ✧
Sr. Margaret Mach

The publishing team for this book included Carl Koch, development editor; Barbara Augustyn Sirovatka, copy editor and typesetter; Joellen Barak Ramer, production editor; Elaine Kohner, illustrator; pre-press, printing, and binding by the graphics division of Saint Mary's Press.

The scriptural quotations on pages 37 and 65 are from the New Revised Standard Version of the Bible. Copyright © 1989 by the Division of Christian Education of the National Council of the Churches of Christ in the United States of America. All rights reserved.
The scriptural material found on pages 60, 99, and 105 is freely adapted and is not to be understood or used as an official translation of the Bible.
The psalm on page 81 is from *Psalms Anew: In Inclusive Language*, compiled by Nancy Schreck and Maureen Leach (Winona, MN: Saint Mary's Press, 1986), pages 40–41. Copyright © 1986 by Saint Mary's Press. All rights reserved.
All of the other scriptural quotations used in this book are from the New Jerusalem Bible. Copyright © 1985 by Darton, Longman & Todd,Ltd., London; and Doubleday, a division of Bantam, Doubleday, Dell Publishing Group, New York. Used with permission.

The acknowledgments continue on page 122.

Printed in the United States of America

Printing: 9 8 7 6 5 4 3

Year: 2002 01 00 1999 98 97 96

ISBN 0-88489-303-0

2767

✧ Contents ✧

✧ Foreword ✧

Companions for the Journey

Just as food is required for human life, so are companions. Indeed, the word *companions* comes from two Latin words: *com*, meaning "with," and *panis*, meaning "bread." Companions nourish our heart, mind, soul, and body. They are also the people with whom we can celebrate the sharing of bread.

Perhaps the most touching stories in the Bible are about companionship: the Last Supper, the wedding feast at Cana, the sharing of the loaves and the fishes, and Jesus' breaking of bread with the disciples on the road to Emmaus. Each incident of companionship with Jesus revealed more about his mercy, love, wisdom, suffering, and hope. When Jesus went to pray in the Garden of Olives, he craved the companionship of the Apostles. They let him down. But God sent the Spirit to inflame the hearts of the Apostles, and they became faithful companions to Jesus and to one another.

Throughout history, other faithful companions have followed Jesus and the Apostles. These saints and mystics have also taken the journey from conversion, through suffering, to resurrection. Just as they were inspired by the holy people who went before them, so too may you take them as your companions as you walk on your spiritual journey.

The Companions for the Journey series is a response to the spiritual hunger of Christians. This series makes available the rich spiritual teachings of mystics and guides whose wisdom can help us on our pilgrimages. As you complete the last meditation in each volume, it is hoped that you will feel supported, challenged, and affirmed by a soul-companion on your spiritual journey.

The spiritual hunger that has emerged over the last twenty years is a great sign of renewal in Christian life. People fill retreat programs and workshops on topics in spirituality. The demand for spiritual directors exceeds the number available. Interest in the lives and writings of saints and mystics is increasing as people search for models of whole and holy Christian life.

Praying with Thomas Merton

Praying with Thomas Merton is more than just a book about Merton's spirituality. This book seeks to engage you in praying in the way that Merton did about issues and themes that were central to his experience. Each meditation can enlighten your understanding of his spirituality and lead you to reflect on your own experience.

The goal of *Praying with Thomas Merton* is that you will discover Merton's rich spirituality and integrate his spirit and wisdom into your relationship with God, with your brothers and sisters, and with your own heart and mind.

Suggestions for Praying with Thomas Merton

Meet Thomas Merton, a fascinating companion for your pilgrimage, by reading the introduction to this book, which begins on page 15. It provides a brief biography of Merton and an outline of the major themes of his spirituality.

Once you meet Thomas Merton, you will be ready to pray with him and to encounter God, your sisters and brothers, and yourself in new and wonderful ways. To help your prayer, here are some suggestions that have been part of the tradition of Christian spirituality:

Create a sacred space. Jesus said, "'When you pray, go to your private room, shut yourself in, and so pray to your [God] who is in that secret place, and your [God] who sees all that is done in secret will reward you'" (Matthew 6:6). Solitary prayer is best done in a place where you can have privacy and silence, both of which can be luxuries in the life of busy people.

If privacy and silence are not possible, create a quiet, safe place within yourself, perhaps while riding to and from work, while sitting in line at the dentist's office, or while waiting for someone. Do the best you can, knowing that a loving God is present everywhere. Whether the meditations in this book are used for solitary prayer or with a group, try to create a prayerful mood with candles, meditative music, an open Bible, or a crucifix.

Open yourself to the power of prayer. Every human experience has a religious dimension. All of life is suffused with God's presence. So remind yourself that God is present as you begin your period of prayer. Do not worry about distractions. If something keeps intruding during your prayer, spend some time talking with God about it. Be flexible because God's Spirit blows where it will.

Prayer can open your mind and widen your vision. Be open to new ways of seeing God, people, and yourself. As you open yourself to the Spirit of God, different emotions are evoked, such as sadness from tender memories, or joy from a celebration recalled. Our emotions are messages from God that can tell us much about our spiritual quest. Also, prayer strengthens our will to act. Through prayer, God can touch our will and empower us to live according to what we know is true.

Finally, many of the meditations in this book will call you to employ your memories, your imagination, and the circumstances of your life as subjects for prayer. The great mystics and saints realized that they had to use all their resources to know God better. Indeed, God speaks to us continually and touches us constantly. We must learn to listen and feel with all the means that God has given us.

Come to prayer with an open mind, heart, and will.

Preview each meditation before beginning. After you have placed yourself in God's presence, spend a few moments previewing the readings and especially the reflection activities. Several reflection activities are given in each meditation because different styles of prayer appeal to different personalities or personal needs. **Note that each meditation has more**

reflection activities than can be done during one prayer period. Therefore, select only one or two reflection activities each time you use a meditation. Do not feel compelled to complete all the reflection activities.

Read meditatively. Each meditation offers you a story about Thomas Merton and a reading from his writings. Take your time reading. If a particular phrase touches you, stay with it. Relish its feelings, meanings, and concerns.

Use the reflections. Following the readings is a short reflection in commentary form, which is meant to give perspective to the readings. Then you are offered several ways of meditating on the readings and the theme of the prayer. You may be familiar with the different methods of meditating, but in case you are not, they are described briefly here:

✦ *Repeated short prayer or mantra:* One means of focusing your prayer is to use a mantra, or "prayer word." The mantra may be a single word or a short phrase taken from the readings or from the Scriptures. For example, a short prayer for meditation 1 in this book is simply the phrase "fire of love." Repeated slowly in harmony with your breathing, the mantra helps you center your heart and mind on one action or attribute of God.

✦ *Lectio divina:* This type of meditation is "divine studying," a concentrated reflection on the word of God or the wisdom of a spiritual writer. Most often in *lectio divina,* you will be invited to read one of the passages several times and then concentrate on one or two sentences, pondering their meaning for you and their effect on you. *Lectio divina* commonly ends with formulation of a resolution.

✦ *Guided meditation:* In this type of meditation, our imagination helps us consider alternative actions and likely consequences. Our imagination helps us experience new ways of seeing God, our neighbors, ourselves, and nature. When Jesus told his followers parables and stories, he engaged their imagination. In this book, you will be invited to follow guided meditations.

One way of doing a guided meditation is to read the scene or story several times, until you know the outline and can recall it when you enter into reflection. Or before your prayer time, you may wish to record the meditation on a tape recorder. If so, remember to allow pauses for reflection between phrases and to speak with a slow, peaceful pace and tone. Then, during prayer, when you have finished the readings and the reflection commentary, you can turn on your recording of the meditation and be led through it. If you find your own voice too distracting, ask a friend to make the tape for you.

✦ *Examen of consciousness:* The reflections often will ask you to examine how God has been speaking to you in your past and present experience—in other words, the reflections will ask you to examine your awareness of God's presence in your life.

✦ *Journal writing:* Writing is a process of discovery. If you write for any length of time, stating honestly what is on your mind and in your heart, you will unearth much about who you are, how you stand with your God, what deep longings reside in your soul, and more. In some reflections, you will be asked to write a dialog with Jesus or someone else. If you have never used writing as a means of meditation, try it. Reserve a special notebook for your journal writing. If desired, you can go back to your entries at a future time for an examen of consciousness.

✦ *Action:* Occasionally, a reflection will suggest singing a favorite hymn, going out for a walk, or undertaking some other physical activity. Action, particularly service to your neighbor, can be a meaningful form of prayer.

Using the Meditations for Group Prayer

If you wish to use the meditations for community prayer, these suggestions may help:

✦ Read the theme to the group. Call the community into the presence of God, using the short opening prayer. Invite one or two participants to read one or both readings. If you use both readings, observe the pause between them.

✦ The reflection commentary may be used as a reading, or it can be deleted, depending on the needs and interests of the group.

✦ Select one of the reflection activities for your group. Allow sufficient time for your group to reflect, to recite a centering prayer or mantra, to accomplish a studying prayer (*lectio divina*), or to finish an examen of consciousness. Depending on the group and the amount of available time, you may want to invite the participants to share their reflections, responses, or petitions with the group.

✦ Reading the passage from the Scriptures may serve as a summary of the meditation.

✦ If a formulated prayer or a psalm is given as a closing, it may be recited by the entire group. Or you may ask participants to offer their own prayers for the closing.

Now you are ready to begin praying with Thomas Merton, a faithful and caring companion on this stage of your spiritual journey. It is hoped that you will find him to be a true soul-companion.

CARL KOCH,
Editor

Note: Thomas Merton died before inclusive language came into general use. Because changing Merton's words would be intrusive in the extreme, the passages have been unaltered. However, given his commitment to justice, Merton would have approved of and employed inclusive language in his writing.

✧ Preface ✧

This book on Thomas Merton has allowed me to share some of my enthusiasm for a spiritual master who has guided me through the years. I am deeply grateful to Thomas Merton for his ongoing influence on my life and prayer.

I owe a tremendous debt to the talented Merton scholars who read and edited the earliest chapters of this book: Robert E. Daggy, curator of the Thomas Merton Center, for kindly advice and resources; Patrick O'Connell, professor of theology at Gannon University, for his perceptive critique and enthusiastic support; Donna Kristoff, OSU, artist and professor, for her hospitality and thorough review; and Br. Patrick Hart, Abbey of Gethsemani, who warmly welcomed my request for help.

Special thanks are due to Carl Koch, FSC, editor of the Companions for the Journey series, whose comments and assistance were invaluable.

Finally, I am grateful for the encouragement and creative contribution of all those who have listened to my talks and attended my retreats on Thomas Merton.

WAYNE SIMSIC

✧ Introduction ✧

Thomas Merton:
The Way of the Contemplative

Thomas Merton, a twentieth-century Trappist monk, wrote passionately about spirituality and mysticism in a way that speaks to the needs of women and men today.

In his outpouring of books and articles, Merton explored the Desert Fathers, Christian mysticism, modern psychology, Catholic, Byzantine, and Protestant theology, Eastern religions, Zen, art, poetry, literature, existentialism, and social issues. His writings uniquely blend monastic tradition and contemporary concerns. Merton's work reveals a person enthusiastic about the spiritual adventure and passionate about union with God through prayer.

Thomas Merton's gift to all of us is this simple message: the contemplative experience, which leads to a unique unity with the divine and a new vision of life, is not only for monks but for all Christians. He remarked: "My vocation is rare perhaps, but contemplation does not exist only within the walls of the cloister. Every man, to live a life full of significance, is called simply to know the significant interior of life and to find ultimate significance in its proper inscrutable existence, in spite of himself, in spite of the world and appearances, in the Living God" (*Honorable Reader: Reflections on My Work*, p. 39).

This Trappist monk, even during the three years he lived in his hermitage, communicated with men and women from all walks of life and from a variety of cultures and religions. Most felt that he was personally addressing their deepest needs. Though he never wanted a following, Thomas Merton became one of the best loved and most influential spiritual masters of our time.

Early Years

Thomas Merton was born on 31 January 1915 at Prades in the French Pyrenees. His parents, Owen and Ruth, had met while studying in Paris under the same English painter, fallen in love, married, and moved to the south of France where they could live simply and dedicate themselves to painting. But during the First World War, the family moved to Long Island where John Paul, Thomas's only sibling, was born.

Although Owen was an accomplished landscape water-colorist, he could not support a wife and children solely by his art. He took other jobs, and the family lived frugally. An independent-minded New Zealand Anglican, Owen acted according to his beliefs.

Merton always remembered the high expectations that his mother, Ruth, had for him and his inability to live up to them as a child. When he was only six, Ruth died of cancer. Shortly before dying, she wrote a letter to Tom, telling him that she would never see him again. With her death, Tom's childhood world collapsed. This tragedy loosened his ties to a strong center and set the young boy adrift on a pilgrimage that would continue for the rest of his life.

After Ruth's death, Owen sometimes took Tom on his painting expeditions. Once they went to Provincetown, Cape Cod, where Tom played on the decks of schooners. On another trip to Bermuda, the seven-year-old boy marveled at the sheer beauty of the island and sea. Drawn together because of their mutual loss, father and son shared a special closeness during these trips.

Apart from these trips, Tom and John Paul settled into family life with their grandparents, Sam and Martha Jenkins, in Douglastown, Long Island. Owen went away for a long period to paint, traveling to Algeria and the south of France. When Owen returned, he told Tom that he wanted to take him back to France with him. By this time the boy had found stability and companionship and was enjoying activities like swimming and baseball. A new home was the last thing Tom wanted. Although he was against the move, Tom found the time spent in France to be an important formative experience.

In France, Tom roamed among old churches and monasteries, fascinated by the relics of the medieval culture. He began his studies at the Lycée Ingres at Montauban. The two years there were a dark period for the eleven-year-old boy. Besides coping with bullying, foul-mouthed students, Tom had to deal with feelings of fear and abandonment.

To Tom's great relief, Owen decided to move to England. In 1928, Tom entered Ripley Court, a small boys' boarding school near London. He had to join the lowest class because he did not know Latin. But in little more than a year, Tom caught up with his age-group and passed the entrance exam for Oakham Public School, where he would spend four years preparing for college.

In the summer of 1929, tragedy struck Tom again. Owen entered a hospital in London and, after a prolonged struggle, died of a malignant brain tumor only days before Tom's sixteenth birthday. Witnessing his father's growing helplessness tore Tom apart. Depressed, unable to make sense out of his father's death and the drawn out suffering that it entailed, another question haunted the young man: Where would he find his home now?

After Owen's death, Tom spent his school holidays with Tom Bennett, his father's doctor and wealthy friend. Bennett became Tom's guardian, father figure, intellectual model, and tutor in the ways of the world. Generous and kind, Bennett encouraged the young man's reading and appreciation of film and art history. Tom continued at Oakham School in England and spent summers with his grandparents on Long Island.

Tom rejected institutional religion, insisting that he believed in nothing. When he could, Tom wandered around Europe, alone. During one of these trips, he developed blood poisoning. Of this time of depression and aimlessness, Merton later wrote in his autobiography: "And I lay there with nothing in my heart but apathy—there was a kind of pride and spite in it: as if it was life's fault that I had to suffer a little discomfort, and for that I would show my scorn and hatred of life, and die" (*The Seven Storey Mountain*, p. 97).

Then life seemed to take an upswing. In 1932, Tom won a scholarship to Clare College, Cambridge. He entertained dreams of dressing well, dating, talking with intellectuals, writing, singing, and playing squash and tennis.

Just after celebrating his eighteenth birthday, Tom used a gift of tickets and money from Bennett to travel across France and to Rome. On his meanderings through early Christian churches and basilicas, he became fascinated by the splendid Byzantine mosaics. It dawned on Tom that he had become a pilgrim who saw in the Byzantine crucifixes something that he had been searching for: "I was unconsciously and unintentionally visiting all the great shrines of Rome, and seeking out their sanctuaries with some of the eagerness and avidity and desire of a true pilgrim" (*Seven Storey Mountain*, p. 108).

Tom began to pray and read from his newly purchased Bible. Then he received a vision. He felt his father's presence in his room: "The whole thing passed in a flash, but in that flash, instantly, I was overwhelmed with a sudden and profound insight into the misery and corruption of my own soul" (*Seven Storey Mountain*, p. 111).

Although Merton described this event in his autobiography from the perspective of a zealous monk looking back on the follies of youth, the experience proved to be a dramatic spiritual turning point: "The one thing that seems to me morally certain is that this was really a grace, and a great grace. If I had only followed it through, my life might have been very different and much less miserable for the years that were to come" (*Seven Storey Mountain*, p. 112).

Cambridge and Columbia

Thomas Merton began classes at Clare College, Cambridge, in October 1933 with the intent of entering the British diplomatic corps. However, he cut classes, studied subjects he chose rather than the ones required, and drank alcohol. He fathered a child, and evidently a paternity suit was filed against him. With the help of his guardian, Tom accepted responsibility for the child and worked out an arrangement. Virtually nothing is known of the woman and child, although Merton left a part of his assets to them when he entered the monastery.

Profoundly disappointed by Tom's irresponsible lifestyle and sexual exploits, Bennett summoned him to London. He told Tom that he had better return to the United States. Deeply ashamed, Tom had no defense for his behavior. A short time later, he was removed from Cambridge and sent on a merchant ship back to his mother's parents in New York. On the voyage, Tom had time to think about his troubled life, his betrayal of his father's expectations for him, and his own sense of worthlessness.

Taking up residence with his grandparents, Tom enrolled at Columbia University, where his boundless enthusiasm for life found direction and flourished. Still a dedicated fraternity man as well as a hard drinker and smoker, he was unconsciously driven to seek a way to fill the frightening abyss he felt at the core of his being.

At Columbia, Tom came under the influence of bright, concerned friends—Bob Lax, Ed Rice, and Sy Freedgood. Literature professor Mark Van Doren inspired him to an authentic search for the truth, and philosopher Daniel Walsh, who kept in touch with Merton throughout his life, became a spiritual confidant. Looking back over the influence of these people on his pilgrimage, Merton comments in *The Seven Storey Mountain*: "God brought me and a half dozen others together at Columbia, and made us friends, in such a way that our friendship would work powerfully to rescue us from the confusion and the misery in which we had come to find ourselves" (p. 178).

Tom's reading and experience directed him more and more to the Catholic faith. His friend Bramachari, the Hindu monk, suggested Tom read *The Confessions of Saint Augustine* and *The Imitation of Christ*. Authors like Etienne Gilson, Aldous Huxley, William Blake, and Jacques Maritain expanded his image of God and the varieties of religious experience. Gradually Tom realized that "books and ideas and poems and stories, pictures and music, buildings, cities, places, philosophies were to be the materials on which grace would work" (*Seven Storey Mountain*, p. 178). He felt that his entire life was being pulled toward God.

Tom found the courage to see a priest and started to attend Mass. Then one day, while reading the life story of Jesuit poet Gerard Manley Hopkins, Tom realized that his own inner life was crying out for a commitment. He tried to ignore these stirrings, but they became even more intense. He put down the book, walked several blocks from the Columbia campus to the Church of Corpus Christi rectory, and asked to become a Catholic.

On 16 November 1938, several friends from Columbia witnessed Thomas Merton's baptism into the Catholic church. After years of searching, he had made a decision to allow Christ to offer him peace and a new reality.

Becoming a Trappist Monk

Merton received his master's degree in literature in 1939 and made plans to study for a doctorate. He spent time with friends, wrote poems and experimental novels, listened to jazz, and traveled. Merton found that his new religious belief had changed his vision, allowing him to experience the deepest peace and happiness he had ever known. However, one question haunted him in the midst of his newfound joy: Should he become a priest?

Merton responded to this new self-awareness with his usual innate romanticism. His mentor, Daniel Walsh, talked to Merton about the Trappists. On hearing of their way of life, Merton said that he "had no desire to join it. . . . The very title made me shiver" (*Seven Storey Mountain*, pp. 262–263). Merton envisioned himself as a Franciscan, living a life of joy, poverty, and simplicity.

He visited the Franciscans. Overcome with a sense of unworthiness, he described the sins of his past life to the Franciscan priest who interviewed him. After hearing about the paternity suit, the priest counseled Merton to withdraw his application. Deeply disappointed, Merton concluded: "The only thing I knew, besides my own tremendous misery, was that I must no longer consider that I had a vocation to the cloister" (*Seven Storey Mountain*, p. 298).

Merton took a position in the English department at Saint Bonaventure College. He followed a rigorous schedule of prayer, liturgy, spiritual reading, and solitary walks. Life was good, peaceful. During his first year of teaching, Merton spent

Holy Week in retreat at the Abbey of Our Lady of Gethsemani in Kentucky. The retreat only intensified his longings for God, and he left Gethsemani wondering whether God was calling him to be a Trappist monk after all.

Back at Saint Bonaventure's, Merton heard the Baroness Catherine de Hueck speak about her work with poor people in Harlem. Merton wondered if the settlement house founded by de Hueck might be a good alternative to the monastic life. He wrote her: "This letter is to let you know that, in me, you are getting no bargain. . . . I am not only not a Saint but just a weak, proud, self-centered little guy, interested in writing, who wants to belong to God, and who, incidentally, was once in a scandal" (William H. Shannon, ed., *The Hidden Ground of Love: The Letters of Thomas Merton*, p. 9). Friendship House in Harlem opened a new world to Merton, a world of poverty and dehumanization. His own emptiness and spiritual uneasiness intensified his identification with the needy people served by the house.

A stark choice confronted Merton: Harlem or Gethsemani? He prayed, and the choice became clearer. He asked a priest if any canonical impediment stood in his way. The priest advised Merton to seek advice from the abbot of Gethsemani. Merton wrote to the abbot, asking to make a Christmas retreat and hinting at his desire to enter the postulancy. While waiting for the abbot's reply, Merton received his military draft notice, advising him to report for induction. However, Merton's heart was leading him to Gethsemani. He decided to go, hoping that the monastery would accept him. On 9 December 1941, he boarded the train for Kentucky.

> Mile after mile my desire to be in the monastery increased beyond belief. . . . What if they did not receive me? Then I would go to the army. But surely that would be a disaster? Not at all. If, after all this, I was rejected by the monastery and had to be drafted, it would be quite clear that it was God's will. I had done everything that was in my power; the rest was in His hands. . . .
>
> I was free. I had recovered my liberty. I belonged to God, not to myself: and to belong to Him is to be free. (*Seven Storey Mountain*, p. 370)

The Trappist Monastery of Gethsemani

Merton stayed in the monastery guest house, waiting for his acceptance. When word came that he could enter the community, even the bare, unheated buildings could not blunt his spiritual enthusiasm. He willingly renounced his name (taking the religious name of Louis), all his worldly possessions, and (in his mind) his writing.

The Trappists, formally known as the Cistercian Order of the Strict Observance, form the most austere community that follows the Benedictine rule. Trappist communities are dedicated to silence and contemplation. Merton ate food, dressed in clothes, and followed religious practices that were medieval in origin. He lived a life of simplicity, routine, silence (communicating through sign language), confinement, hard work, and prayer in a community of over one hundred monks. He responded with joyful enthusiasm. For the first time in his life, Merton felt genuinely at home. He would later recall his years in the novitiate as physically hard but mentally happy.

Merton found peace in the new ordering of his life, the deep silence and solitude, and the physical beauty of the countryside. However, he discovered that outward changes did not tamp the fires of his active intellect or curb his need to express a fertile imagination.

Merton's brother, John Paul, visited and was baptized before going overseas as a member of the Royal Canadian Air Force. In spring of the following year, Merton received news that his brother's plane had been shot down in the North Sea. He wrote a poem, "For My Brother: Reported Missing in Action, 1943," to express his sorrow:

> Sweet brother, if I do not sleep
> My eyes are flowers for your tomb;
> And if I cannot eat my bread,
> My fasts shall live like willows where you died. . . .
>
> (*Seven Storey Mountain*, p. 404)

Merton felt the urge to write, but he agonized over the suitability of writing in the life of a contemplative monk. Merton the writer continued to think of possible books, while Merton the contemplative wanted to give up writing.

Merton the monk turned the dilemma over to his superiors. They told him to write. Merton began by writing poems and short books on Cistercian life. Then in 1946, he started writing his autobiography, *The Seven Storey Mountain.*

In a private journal (eventually published as *The Sign of Jonas*), Merton referred to himself as "Jonas," identifying with the prophet who struggled with conflicting desires. As the time for his final vows approached, he not only struggled with being a writer in a monastery but also wondered whether the Trappists' contemplative life was too active for him. Would he be happier in an order like the Carthusians that had fewer hours of work and public prayer and more opportunity for solitude and private prayer?

In 1948, Abbot James Fox, aware of Merton's need for solitude, allowed him to spend part of each Sunday in the woods. Later, as the monastery's modern farm equipment increased the noise level, he offered Merton a vault and eventually a tool shed in the woods in which to write. Merton called the shed Saint Anne's Hermitage. It seemed to be the solution he was looking for, yet Merton continued to explore the possibility of even greater solitude.

The publication of *The Seven Storey Mountain* in 1948 and its enormous popularity changed Merton's life and heightened the tension between writing and contemplative living. Reflecting the theological outlook of 1940s Catholicism and Merton's youthful idealism, the book became a national best-seller and has remained in print ever since. Its success brought international attention to the Trappist monastery isolated in rural Kentucky. Suddenly men besieged Gethsemani, wanting to become Trappists. Merton's story inspired people of all ages, and fan mail poured in. Merton started accepting himself as a Trappist monk who was also a writer.

However, shortly before his ordination, Merton's doubts about himself returned. He felt paralyzed, unable to pray or to write. He made the following journal entry the day before he was ordained: "My life is a great mess and tangle of half-conscious subterfuges to evade grace and duty. . . . My infidelity to Christ, instead of making me sick with despair, drives me to throw myself all the more blindly into the arms of His mercy" (*The Sign of Jonas* [1956], pp. 190–191). He persevered in this period of darkness and discovered a renewed peace. Thomas Merton became Father Louis on 26 May 1949.

"Guilty Bystander"

Despite periods of exhaustion, illness, and time in the infirmary, the next years were fruitful for Merton. He finished three books of meditations: *New Seeds of Contemplation, No Man Is an Island,* and *Thoughts in Solitude.*

In June 1951, Merton was appointed master of scholastics, which meant that he would direct the spiritual growth and study of young professed monks. This new responsibility greatly limited Merton's time. He made this observation: "I stand on the threshold of a new existence. The one who is going to be most fully formed by the new scholasticate is the Master of Scholastics" (*Sign of Jonas* [1956], p. 319). Even so, he continued his writing, and the realization that the contemplative path had to include responsibility and compassion for other people deepened within him.

Merton began to take keen interest in the civil rights movement. He closely followed the activities of Martin Luther King, Jr., and, like King, immersed himself in the writings of Gandhi. Indeed, Merton read widely and deeply, as if preparing himself for the next pivotal event of his life.

On 18 March 1958, Merton had a dentist appointment in Louisville, Kentucky. While standing on the corner of Fourth and Walnut Streets, he suddenly became aware of his connection with all people. In a journal he had been writing since 1956, called *Conjectures of a Guilty Bystander,* he tried to describe this revelation: "I was suddenly overwhelmed with the realization that I loved all those people, that they were mine and I theirs, that we could not be alien to one another even though we were total strangers" (p. 156). Standing on that street corner, Merton came to realize that holiness did not require silence, isolation, and renunciation of the world. He knew that his contemplative life had to be touched by and touch the lives of other human beings.

Soon after this revelation, Merton wrote to Dorothy Day, cofounder of the Catholic Worker movement, expressing his appreciation for her ministry and his need for solidarity with the poor:

> You people are . . . among the few that still have an eye open. I am more and more convinced that the real people in this country are the Indians—and Negroes, etc. . . . The reason I mention the Hopis is that (this is in confidence) I think more and more that the only final solution to my own desires will be something like getting permission to go off and live among Indians or some such group, as a kind of hermit-missionary. (Shannon, ed., *Hidden Ground of Love*, p. 136)

Though still actively engaged in the life of the monastery, Merton turned more of his attention to matters of justice and peace. In *Conjectures of a Guilty Bystander*, he described himself as a "guilty bystander" in a turbulent, desperate, cynical, and violent world. As one responsible to humankind, Merton ministered to this world through his continued writing.

Against the general tide of Catholic support for government policy toward the Cold War, Merton published articles on nonviolence and peacemaking. He produced a book-sized collection of "Cold War Letters"; however, they were never published together because the abbot general asked Merton to cease writing about such subjects. At first Merton was angered by the directive, but he accepted the silencing, believing that he had already said his piece and that God would use the events in a positive way not apparent at the moment.

Unable to march or even to write about peace issues, Merton brought compassion to the struggle through his influence on activists and others who wrote to or visited him. He contended that the desire for peace is rooted in the spiritual life. He trusted that no good action is wasted, even if results are not immediately evident. At the same time, Merton argued that without the contemplative dimension, any action could go awry.

The turmoil of the sixties started another crescendo. In 1963, John F. Kennedy was assassinated; the Harlem riots were only a year away. When the restrictions on Merton's publications were lifted, he issued *Seeds of Destruction*. He was also working on a small book, *Gandhi on Non-Violence*, which dem-

demonstrated that Gandhi's principles remain as relevant today as when they were conceived and practiced in India.

Merton opposed the Vietnam war and nurtured an acute awareness of other social problems. As a young man, Merton had taken refuge from the world in order to find union with God. Now he realized that the intense struggle for this union called him to engage with the world to work for peace and equality among his brothers and sisters.

Hermitage Years

In August 1965, Abbot Dom James gave Merton permission to live as a full-time hermit in a cinder block cottage set on a knoll not quite a mile from the abbey. The cottage was originally constructed for meetings with ecumenical groups. Merton acknowledged that while most monks found the traditional monastic silence "sufficient," a few needed the solitary life that was to him "the crown of the monastic vocation" (*The Monastic Journey*, p. 179).

As he settled in and immersed himself in studying mystics such as Julian of Norwich, Merton realized that he was at a crucial stage in his spiritual journey. Shortly after his fiftieth birthday, Merton took stock of his life, especially his call to solitude. "Over and over again, I see that this life is what I have always hoped it would be and always sought. It is a life of peace, silence, purpose and meaning" (*A Vow of Conversation: Journals 1964–1965*, p. 206). Merton also realized that solitude tears off masks and tolerates no lies.

On an ordinary day, Merton prayed, meditated, swept, cleaned, cut wood, and wrote. He celebrated Mass at the monastery, but he took his meals at the hermitage (eventually a chapel was added to the hermitage). Merton suffered from dermatitis, had surgery for bursitis, and was troubled by allergies. When he discovered that the stream from which he had been drawing water was polluted, he had to carry water to the hermitage. Despite these inconveniences, Merton cherished the time to walk in the woods before daybreak and the hours in uninterrupted prayer.

This hermit with various ailments and a sense of humor continued to cultivate hospitality and friendship with a wide variety of people. Scholars, peace activists, writers, theologians, and friends visited Merton at his hermitage.

Merton retained his interest in monastic renewal. For instance, many of his essays from *Contemplation in a World of Action* and *The Monastic Journey* address such questions as "What does it mean to be a monk?" and "How does a monk live in the twentieth century?" Merton questioned a monastic obedience that emphasized institutional control rather than life ordered toward seeking God. He also concluded: "The monastery is not an 'escape' from the world. On the contrary, by being in the monastery I take my true part in all the struggles and sufferings of the world" (*Honorable Reader*, "Preface to Japanese edition of *Seven Storey Mountain*," p. 65).

Traveling East

Merton had a long-standing interest in other Christian communities and in other religions. He thought that sharing religious experiences nurtured world unity and peace. Merton recognized that God belongs not solely to Christians, and he regularly corresponded with Jews, Buddhists, and Muslims.

Eastern religions, especially Zen Buddhism, intrigued Merton. *Zen and the Birds of Appetite* and *Mystics and Zen Masters* contain many of his essays on Zen. A 1964 visit with Daisetsu T. Suzuki, a Zen scholar, revived Merton's interest in Chuang Tzu, the Chinese sage. Merton took particular delight in translating a group of Taoist poems, published as *The Way of Chuang Tzu*, because they so accurately mirrored his own spiritual concerns.

Merton thrived on interreligious dialog, but he also realized that this exchange had its limitations. So when he received an invitation to travel to the Far East and take part in a conference on monastic experience and East-West dialog, Merton sought and received the permission of his new abbot, Dom Flavian Burns, to go. Because of a deep solidarity with Asian monastics, he saw himself as a humble pilgrim, open to revelation. Having knocked on the door of the East in his imagination and his heart, he was now ready to enter deeper into its mystery. In Merton's mind, all aspects of this trip pointed homeward.

Final Pilgrimage

Merton told the story of his pilgrimage to the East in *The Asian Journal*. He traveled extensively—New Delhi, Calcutta, Darjeeling—and met a number of sages. Among these were the Dalai Lama, who was struck by Merton's humility and spirituality, and Chatral Rimpoche, who called Merton a "natural Buddha." Merton journeyed to Sri Lanka and then back to Bangkok.

He had set out as a wisdom seeker, not as a renowned figure: "I come as a pilgrim who is anxious to obtain not just information, not just 'facts' about other monastic traditions, but to drink from ancient sources of monastic vision and experience" (Naomi Burton, Patrick Hart, and James Laughlin, eds., *The Asian Journal of Thomas Merton*, p. 312). People, whether cab drivers, monks, or nuns, immediately responded to his intellect, his charm, and his spirituality.

While in Sri Lanka visiting the colossal Buddha figures carved out of rock, Merton had another focal experience. He wrote: "I don't know when in my life I have ever had such a sense of beauty and spiritual validity running together in one aesthetic illumination" (Burton, Hart, and Laughlin, eds., *Asian Journal*, p. 235). This moment of aesthetic-mystical enlightenment clarified Merton's vision, allowing him to see beyond surfaces, beyond the illusion that surrounded reality.

On 10 December 1968, Merton gave his final talk at a Bangkok conference. His paper, entitled "Marxism and Monastic Perspectives," had preoccupied him for weeks. In it he suggests that both Marxism and monasticism urge change in the world: Marx, a revolution of the economic structure; monasticism, a transformation of consciousness. Merton's thesis: Inner transformation is at the heart of the monastic vow.

At about 4:00 p.m., during the recess following Merton's presentation, a priest went to check on him. He found Merton dead, apparently electrocuted by a defective fan.

The icon Merton had with him when he died contained these words: "If we wish to please the true God and to be friends with the most blessed of friendships, let us present our spirit naked to God." Merton's body was flown back to the United States in the company of Americans killed in the Vietnam war, the very war he had protested.

After a funeral Mass at Gethsemani attended by lay and religious friends, his brother monks buried Merton in a small cemetery next to the abbey church. At the end of the service, the following words were read from the conclusion of *The Seven Storey Mountain*:

> But you shall taste the true solitude of my anguish and my poverty and I shall lead you into the high places of my joy and you shall die in Me and find all things in My mercy which has created you for this end and brought you from Prades to Bermuda to St. Antonin to Oakham to London to Cambridge to Rome to New York to Columbia

to Corpus Christi to St. Bonaventure to the Cistercian Abbey of the poor men who labor in Gethsemani:

That you may become the brother of God and learn to know the Christ of the burnt men. (Pp. 422–423)

Merton's Spirituality

Neatly summarizing Merton's spirituality is impossible because he does not present a systematic treatment on any given subject. His vision threaded itself through notebooks, journals, autobiographical reflections, and private correspondence. His language is often that of metaphor, symbol, and image.

Thomas Merton's spirituality was shaped in the variety of events, tensions, and paradoxes of his life. If any one statement captures the essence of Merton's spirituality, perhaps it is this one: "All life tends to grow like this, in mystery inscaped with paradox and contradiction, yet centered, in its very heart, on the divine mercy" (Thomas P. McDonnell, ed., *A Thomas Merton Reader*, p. 17).

The following are of some key characteristics of Merton's vision:

Pilgrimage: Merton saw himself as a pilgrim seeking God beyond the boundaries of the self and of social convention. The more Merton experienced the spiritual journey, the more he realized that he would always be on the road toward the divine mystery.

The monastic life: To view the world as Merton saw it is to view it through the eyes of a monk—a monk with an extraordinary vision, but a monk nevertheless. Merton the monk desired above all else to live out his faith according to the Gospel of Jesus Christ. Monastic life centers on conversion and change of heart, and it flowers in the desert experience.

Solitude: Merton explored the dimensions of solitude in order to discover God and his true self in the purifying yet illuminating darkness of dread, poverty, mystery, and transformation. He sought silence and solitude to experience oneness with God in love and contemplation. Merton claimed that all of us are ultimately solitary, but because we fear aloneness, we try to forget this fact.

The path of darkness and emptiness: Merton willingly embraced the wilderness of the human spirit where he came face to face with his own sinfulness, vulnerability, ignorance, and total dependence on God. He realized that it is essential to empty oneself in order to be filled by God.

Importance of prayer: Merton saw the need to integrate the senses and the body into the prayer experience. Prayer flows out of life, and the goal is to allow our entire lives to become living communion with God and with all creation. For Merton, contemplative prayer was "not so much a way to find God as a way of resting in him whom we have *found*, who loves us, who is near to us, who comes to us to draw us to himself" (*Contemplative Prayer*, p. 29). A person who prays with the heart finds revelation in the concrete realities of one's talents, friends, work, body, and environment.

Mystery of the self: Merton said that we long to awaken to the voice within that invites transformation and calls us to freedom from the old self in order to live totally in the spontaneity of the Spirit. Since this inner self is a secret that cannot be studied or coaxed from hiding by techniques, we can only cultivate in ourselves silence, humility, detachment, and purity of heart so that we are ready to witness the surprise of God's presence.

Quest for true freedom: Merton yearned to free his life from the clutter, distractions, and artificial needs that rob one of freedom, so that he could see and respond to reality and trust in God alone: "The monk is . . . a man who has responded to an authentic call of God to a life of freedom and detachment, a 'desert life' outside normal social structures" (*Contemplation in a World of Action*, p. 26).

Prophetic vocation: Merton said that when we draw close to God, when we experience the purifying, illuminating, transforming experience of God, our life will bear witness to a supreme liberty and draw others toward it.

Social concern: As the contemplative dimension of his life matured, Merton realized that he could not remain separate from the world or reject it. The deepest prayer, he believes, becomes a wellspring for apostolic activity. According to Merton, the greatest danger facing Christians today is the tendency to ignore inner life and become involved in "pseudo-activism," activity not grounded in prayer.

The centrality of Christ: Merton's monastic life, focused on Christ, was directed toward participation in Christ's life through liturgical life, scripture, prayer, work, and monastic art: "Our life in Christ is all-sufficient. What we have been calling the 'contemplative life' is a life of awareness that one thing is necessary, that Jesus is alone necessary and that to live for him and in him is all-sufficient" (*Contemplation in Action,* p. 381).

Merton for Today

Thomas Merton offers us a vast wealth of knowledge, wisdom, and spiritual nourishment from his pilgrimage and his contemplative experience as a Trappist monk. He invites us to explore our inner hunger. He sensitizes us to the depths of the universal human spirit. Merton is a "spiritual master" because "he mastered a way of living which is called monastic while, in turn, using his example and his pen as a way of passing on that life to others, both monks . . . and those who were not called to the cloister" (Lawrence S. Cunningham, ed., *Thomas Merton: Spiritual Master,* pp. 47–48).

Thomas Merton is a spiritual master because he invites us down a spiritual path that we can all follow. He reminds us that we can all receive the gift of the contemplative experience if we are true to God's call and grace on our own pilgrimage.

✧ Meditation 1 ✧

Turning Back to the True Self

Theme: We are created in God's image and are destined to share in divine life, but we find ourselves exiled from both God and our deepest self. Our heart calls us to return to the Source of All Reality who establishes our true identity and becomes the goal of our life's journey.

Opening prayer: All-loving God, lead me back to you. Form me as I was meant to be—loving, faithful, and filled with hope.

About Merton

Before entering Cambridge University, Thomas Merton traveled to Rome and explored the great shrines and churches. He was surprised at his attraction to these sacred places and to the mosaics and frescoes.

One night, he had an important revelation:

> I was in my room. It was night. The light was on. Suddenly it seemed to me that Father, who had now been dead more than a year, was there with me. The sense of his presence was as vivid and as real and as startling as if he had touched my arm or spoken to me. The whole thing

passed in a flash, but in that flash, instantly, I was over-whelmed with a sudden and profound insight into the misery and corruption of my own soul, and I was pierced deeply with a light that made me realize something of the condition I was in, and I was filled with horror at what I saw, and my whole being rose up in revolt against what was within me, and my soul desired escape and liberation and freedom from all this with an intensity and an urgen-cy unlike anything I had ever known before. And now I think for the first time in my whole life I really began to pray—praying not with my lips and with my intellect and my imagination, but praying out of the very roots of my life and of my being, and praying to the God I had never known. (*Seven Storey Mountain*, p. 111)

Looking back on his dissolute youth, Merton demonstrated his early awareness of a self that was false, selfish, and empty.

As a monk, he realized that his recentering around God would be neither quick nor easy, and this knowledge struck fear in his heart. In his journals he reflected:

It is fear that is driving me into solitude. Love has put drops of terror in my veins and they grow cold in me, suddenly, and make me faint with fear because my heart and my imagination wander away from God into their own private idolatry. It is my iniquity that makes me physically faint and turn to jelly because of the contradic-tion between my nature and my God. (*Sign of Jonas* [1956], p. 248)

Pause: Recall a time in your life when you were living a lie and willingly perpetuated the illusion that you did not need God.

Merton's Words

My false and private self is the one who wants to exist outside the reach of God's will and God's love—outside of reality and outside of life. And such a self cannot help but be an illusion.

We are not very good at recognizing illusions, least of all the ones we cherish about ourselves—the ones we are born with and which feed the roots of sin. For most of the people in the world, there is no greater subjective reality than this false self of theirs, which cannot exist. A life devoted to the cult of this shadow is what is called a life of sin.

. . . The secret of my identity is hidden in the love and mercy of God.

But whatever is in God is really identical with Him, for His infinite simplicity admits no division and no distinction. Therefore I cannot hope to find myself anywhere except in Him.

Ultimately the only way that I can be myself is to become identified with Him in Whom is hidden the reason and fulfillment of my existence. (*New Seeds of Contemplation*, pp. 34–36)

Reflection

Merton believed that we need to affirm and love ourselves, but the "self" we need to affirm and love is often hidden beneath a mask. Too often the self we cultivate is only a disguise, a distortion of our true being, which is made in God's image and likeness.

The false self is the one that thinks that it can ultimately control its own fate. The false self is jealous of other people because they are perceived as more beautiful, talented, or intelligent. The false self tries to fill its emptiness by material possessions, but it is never satisfied. The false self tries to satisfy its loneliness and alienation with food, drink, sex, or frantic activity. This shadow self creates a world apart from God and becomes a slave to its own fantasy. It lives a lie because it refuses to recognize its vulnerability without God.

Our true self lets go of any pretense to ultimate control. Our true self embraces our gifts, talents, skills, and body as wonderful graces from a loving God. Our true self seeks only to do the will of God, which is, simply put, "to love." Our true self can rest in God's embrace; our true self is God-likeness seen in the person of Jesus.

Returning to God and our true self means surrendering the false self. It means a conversion in which we put on Christ. It means clothing ourselves in faith, hope, and love—the life for which we were created.

Our false self does not give up easily; conversion seldom happens in the twinkle of an eye. And it is only possible with the grace that God gives freely in Jesus Christ. Even the urgency that prods us to return to God is a gift. We would not seek God unless, as Augustine emphasizes (and Merton with him), we had already been found by God.

We accept the grace of conversion through the practice of humility, silence, and letting go of attachments. This inner transformation continues through contemplative prayer, sometimes described as "a long, loving look at the real" (Walter J. Burghardt, "Contemplation," *Church*, Winter 1989, p. 15). Through "prayer of the heart," the true self sees the illusion of control or envy and becomes aware of itself as separate from the masks and fabrications of an imaginary self. As Merton said: "Contemplation is precisely the awareness that this 'I' is really 'not I' and the awakening of the unknown 'I' that is beyond observation and reflection and is incapable of commenting upon itself" (*New Seeds of Contemplation*, p. 7). According to Merton, we "remember" God through contemplation and at the same time "remember" our identity in God.

One of the signs of God's grace in converting us is that we become aware of God in all aspects of life. We gain a respect for books, work, our body, people, and our surroundings as things that draw us more deeply into God. The journey into the truest self is one that anchors each man and woman more deeply in God and in all life.

✧ Read "About Merton" again and relate his experience of emptiness and inauthenticity to a time when you felt a sense of disgust and despair in your life. Write your reflections in your journal.

Thank God for the "happy faults" that prod you to question the false self and draw you toward life in Christ.

✧ Write a dialog with your false self. Address the self that you recognize as untruthful, a slave to the opinion of others, prone to destructive habits, fearful, anxious, isolated. Express your anger, frustration, and impatience. Give yourself time to hear a reply and continue the dialog as long as you feel the need. End by addressing God and asking for the grace to be aware of the hidden, loving self within.

✧ We need to slow down and step aside in order to be aware of the false "I," which we tend to be satisfied with, and to center ourselves on the true "I" of love.

Close your eyes . . . relax . . . release the tension . . . breathe deeply, slowly, in and out. . . . Now take time to relax each part of your body from your head to your feet. . . . Let your breathing remain slow and rhythmic. . . . Release all need to control.

Now focus on the mystery of yourself, your uniqueness, and your hidden beauty. . . . Take time to be in touch with this self, which feels connected with nature and people and touches on the deepest love you know. . . . Take time to rest in this sense of self.

Offer a prayer that rises spontaneously from your deepest self, the self that loves and wishes to remain in God's presence.

✧ Meditate on the words, "It is no longer I, but Christ living in me" (Galatians 2:20). To allow God's grace to convert you, to draw you back to your true self so that Christ can live in you, what will you have to let go? Write a list of some of the obstacles, attachments, compulsions, and falsehoods that you will have to release in order to turn back to God.

✧ Merton turned to Mary as a sign of the great things God can accomplish in us if we open our heart and choose to remain hidden and poor in spirit. Use Mary's reply to the angel as a mantra, repeating it slowly and gently, allowing it to bring you humbly before God: "Here am I, the servant of the Lord; let it be with me according to your word" (Luke 1:38, NRSV).

✦ What aspects of your life do you encounter with respect, even reverence?

✦ Have you thought of a deepening appreciation of your life as an encounter with your true self?

✦ How can you reinforce the respect and gratitude that you have for certain aspects of your life?

✦ One who prays with the heart can find God in all things; take time to rest in God's love.

God's Word

In the abundance of his glory may [God], through his Spirit, enable you to grow firm in power with regard to your inner self, so that Christ may live in your hearts through faith, and then, planted in love and built on love, with all God's holy people you will have the strength to grasp the breadth and the length, the height and the depth; so that, knowing the love of Christ, which is beyond knowledge, you may be filled with the utter fullness of God. (Ephesians 3:16–19)

Closing prayer: Merciful God, give me the grace to know myself in you and the strength to live a new life in Christ. Teach me how to relax in a simple awareness of your love and to be the person I am in truth.

✧ Meditation 2 ✧

The Search for Freedom

Theme: Inner freedom begins by looking squarely at our enslavement to what is not God: all that is selfish, slovenly, dissolute—in short, sinful. We nourish freedom by discerning God's will and by acting out of our true self.

Opening prayer: O God, guide me through the obstacles and illusions that hinder my journey to the source of all reality and true freedom. Break the shackles of my ignorance, prejudice, and selfishness. Only by burning with your spirit can I truly be free.

About Merton

In the opening paragraph of his autobiography, Thomas Merton looked back on the gift of freedom and his desertion of that freedom:

> On the last day of January 1915, under the sign of the Water Bearer, in a year of a great war, and down in the shadow of some French mountains on the borders of Spain, I came into the world. Free by nature, in the image of God, I was nevertheless the prisoner of my own violence and my own selfishness, in the image of the world into which I was born. (*Seven Storey Mountain*, p. 3)

Merton's enslavement began during his public school and university years. He sought to live without restriction and to follow his desires, considering this to be freedom. He traveled, used his inheritance irresponsibly, and sought both pleasure and passion indiscriminately. After fathering a child, forfeiting his career at Cambridge through irresponsible behavior, and turning his godfather against him, Merton reviewed his past sins during the long voyage across the Atlantic to the United States:

> It did not take very much reflection on the year I had spent at Cambridge to show me that all my dreams of fantastic pleasures and delights were crazy and absurd, and that everything I had reached out for had turned to ashes in my hands, and that I myself, into the bargain, had turned out to be an extremely unpleasant sort of a person—vain, self-centered, dissolute, weak, irresolute, undisciplined, sensual, obscene and proud. I was a mess. (*Seven Storey Mountain*, p. 132)

At age twenty-seven, Merton found his true freedom. Entering the Trappist monastery, he let go of the illusory freedom of his past attachments, values, and comforts. His new freedom came with self-discipline and self-denial. This path of sacrifice gave him the spiritual freedom to love more completely:

> My intention is to give myself entirely and without compromise to whatever work God wants to perform in me and through me. But this gift is not something absolutely blind and without definition. It is already defined by the fact that God has given me a *contemplative* vocation. . . . It means renouncing the business, ambitions, honors and pleasures and other activities of the world. (*Sign of Jonas* [1956], p. 37)

Indeed, following the example of the twelfth-century Cistercian, Saint Bernard, Merton held that freedom is the fundamental aim of the monk: "For St Bernard, the function of the monastery is to liberate man's love from this disastrous illusion [the love for created things as an end in itself] and reorientate it to the one true good, which is God Himself"

(*Monastic Journey*, p. 78). The monastery was Merton's school of freedom, and monastic discipline was the key to liberty. The goal of discipline was charity. By snapping the chain of attachments, a liberated person can give and receive love.

Pause: Consider for a moment your own journey toward greater freedom and the detours that you have taken on that journey.

Merton's Words

I am the utter poverty of God. I am His emptiness, littleness, nothingness, lostness. When this is understood, my life in His freedom, the self-emptying of God in me is the fullness of grace. A love for God that knows no reason because He is the fullness of grace. A love for God that knows no reason because He is God; a love without measure, a love for God as personal. (*Woods, Shore, Desert*, p. 24)

My Lord God, I have no idea where I am going. I do not see the road ahead of me. I cannot know for certain where it will end. Nor do I really know myself, and the fact that I think I am following your will does not mean that I am actually doing so. But I believe that the desire to please you does in fact please you. And I hope I have that desire in all that I am doing. I hope that I will never do anything apart from that desire. And I know that if I do this you will lead me by the right road, though I may know nothing about it. Therefore I will trust you always though I may seem to be lost and in the shadow of death. I will not fear, for you are ever with me, and you will never leave me to face my perils alone. (*Thoughts in Solitude*, p. 81)

Reflection

Merton taught that the lack of freedom is a universal condition from which we need to be delivered. M. Basil Pennington points out that the real question, according to Merton, is not "Am I happy?" but "Am I free?" (*Thomas Merton, Brother Monk,*

p. 15). Original sin abolished the innocence that allowed us to see reality as God sees it. Now we must contend with a multitude of illusions that hide the truth, distort our vision, and enslave us.

Many aspects of society offer an illusion of freedom. For instance, we can choose one product over another. But, manipulated by the tastes and ideas of hucksters and hustlers, losing touch with true freedom becomes all too easy. We are seduced into believing that we can create our own happiness. Like a weed, the false self rises out of the rocky soil of alienation and prevents us from recognizing that our true identity is found in God. The false self, reinforced by self-seeking activities, lulls us into believing that it is real and has substance.

The true self slumbers like a seed planted in fertile ground waiting to be nourished. So when we find ourselves separated from our deepest, truest self and from others, the Spirit within us uses our resentment of the separation, our sense of alienation, and even the resulting anger to draw us back to God. The heart hungers for its true center, its deepest freedom.

The return to freedom requires sacrifice and the ability to say no. Merton taught that "we renounce other forms of freedom in order to have *this* kind of freedom" (*Contemplation in a World of Action*, p. 377). In other words we let go of all that distracts us from or destroys our relationship with God.

Freedom also requires that we say yes—yes, to whatever way God asks us to be free. We listen to God and respond to God's call in the depths of our being. The healing power of Christ's Resurrection has given each man and woman the grace to become a new person in Christ, a whole person no longer dominated by external things, a person empowered by authentic freedom.

✧ Read the prayer in the section "Merton's Words" and recall events that awoke you to the uncertainties of your own life journey. Write a letter to God describing your own sense of being lost and your need for direction.

✧ Allow your mind to wander over the past few days. Think of times when a situation overwhelmed you, and you seemed to lose your freedom. Maybe someone manipulated you into doing something; perhaps you bought an item compulsively. Choose one incident and write your reflections on these questions:

✦ What happened? Who was involved? Why did it happen?
✦ What were my feelings?
✦ What other way could I have handled the situation at the time?
✦ How was I not free, or how did I feel shackled?
✦ What did I learn from this incident?

✧ What is blocking your path to greater inner freedom? Compile a short list. Concentrate on one item on the list and reflect on the way that God is asking you to change your life.

✧ Picture Christ on the cross. Bring the image to mind with as much detail as you can. (If you find it helpful, gaze at a special crucifix or picture of the crucifixion.)

Think of your inability to say yes to God with your entire being. . . . Focus your attention on the gap between yourself and God. . . .

Now return to Jesus on the cross and open yourself to his love, which will fill the empty spaces in you. . . . Ask Jesus for the true freedom that comes from his death and Resurrection.

✧ Light a candle; quiet yourself and relax in the presence of God.

✦ Offer your life to God.
✦ Ask God for the freedom to respond to your truest self.
✦ Thank God for instances when you have said yes to God's grace, yes to loving, yes to God's will.
✦ Pray the Hail Mary, saying the words slowly and pondering your own openness to God.

God's Word

Self-willed people with no reverence . . . are dried-up springs, fogs swirling in the wind, and the gloom of darkness is stored up for them. With their high-sounding but empty talk they tempt back people who have scarcely escaped from those who live in error, by playing on the disordered desires of their human nature and by debaucheries. They may promise freedom but are themselves slaves to corruption; because if anyone [is] dominated by anything, then he [or she] is a slave to it. (2 Peter 2:11, 17–20)

Closing prayer: Liberating God, I know that you love me in spite of my unworthiness. Release me from the chains that bind me and rob me of my freedom. Allow me to become all that you call me to be. May I remain completely open to every manifestation of your love and beauty in my life.

The Gift of Faith

Theme: Becoming a Christian is a lifelong journey, but Jesus Christ keeps us company each step of the way.

Opening prayer: What an awareness—to realize that I receive God's grace as a free gesture of love and that Christ constantly invites me to accept this gift! My God, give me the courage to say yes to this gift and to learn how to utter yes repeatedly throughout my life.

About Merton

The year 1938 proved to be eventful for Thomas Merton. He was baptized and confirmed in the Catholic faith, an event that awakened him to the overwhelming reality of Christ dwelling within him:

> For now I had entered into the everlasting movement of that gravitation which is the very life and spirit of God: God's own gravitation towards the depths of His own infinite nature, His goodness without end. And God, that center Who is everywhere, and whose circumference is nowhere, finding me, through incorporation with Christ, incorporated into this immense and tremendous gravitational movement which is love, which is the Holy Spirit, loved me. (*Seven Storey Mountain*, p. 225)

Merton chose the path of faith because nothing physical or rational filled the void in his life. He awakened to something beyond himself that was worthy of an authentic and complete commitment. For Merton, Roman Catholicism offered a new way of life that satisfied both his intellectual curiosity and his sensitivity to mystery.

Merton took his spiritual quest seriously. He read classical spiritual texts by John of the Cross, Bernard of Clairvaux, Thérèse of Lisieux, Ignatius of Loyola, and many others. These works opened the door to spiritual transformation. An inner urgency steadily drew him toward truth and love.

Merton dreamed of nothing less than holiness. This is best illustrated by a conversation that he had with his friend Bob Lax. While they were walking down Sixth Avenue in New York City, Lax turned to Merton and asked him, "What do you want to be anyway?" Merton thoughtfully replied, "I don't know; I guess what I want is to be a good Catholic." Lax would not let the question rest and suggested that Merton really wanted to be a saint. Acutely aware of his sins, Merton was at first perplexed by his friend's comment. Later, however, he agreed that his friend's observation rang true. (*Seven Storey Mountain*, p. 238)

Merton's conversion to Christ took another dramatic step when he entered Gethsemani. He was at last able to nourish his hungry soul and free his bound spirit. There would be times of doubt and confusion later, but life in the monastery buoyed his spirit and reinforced his faith:

> Love sails me around the house. I walk two steps on the ground and four steps in the air. It is love. It is consolation. I don't care if it is consolation. I am not attached to consolation. I love God. Love carries me all around. I don't want to *do* anything but love. And when the bell rings it is like pulling teeth to make myself shift because of that love, secret love, hidden love, obscure love, down inside me and outside me where I don't care to talk about it. (*Sign of Jonas* [1956], p. 124)

Pause: Consider your own call to intimacy with God. Have you had a time when a door in your heart opened and everything in your life seemed secondary to falling in love with God? What was your response?

Merton's Words

My conversion to the Christian faith, or to be precise my conversion to Christ, is something I have always regarded as a radical liberation from the delusions and obsessions of modern man and his society. I have always believed and continue to believe that faith is the only real protection against the absorption of freedom and intelligence in the crass and thoughtless servitude of mass society. (*Honorable Reader*, p. 64)

Faith is not expected to give complete satisfaction to the intellect. It leaves the intellect suspended in obscurity, without a light proper to its own mode of knowing. Yet it does not frustrate the intellect, or deny it, or destroy it. It pacifies it with a conviction which it knows it can accept quite rationally under the guidance of love. For the act of faith is an act in which the intellect is content to know God by *loving* Him and accepting His statements about Himself on His own terms. (*New Seeds of Contemplation*, pp. 127–128)

Reflection

As Merton's disgust with his lack of focus and sense of meaninglessness grew, he began to admit his need to fill the great void in his life. Merton made a fundamental choice for Christ, but he also realized that this conversion, or turning toward life in God, would involve a lifetime of saying yes to Christ. Conversion is not a once in a lifetime occurrence.

Prayer, reading, and reflection strengthened Merton's ongoing conversion to God in Christ. He also made a series of conscious, often difficult choices that led him to Christ and away from his old life. Entering the monastery, for example, certainly was a dramatic step away from the world he had known and toward the way of Christ. But it was only the beginning.

Conversion certainly does not require that everyone enter a monastery, but it always demands a reordering of our priorities, our sense of self, and our way of life. We choose life grounded in a relationship with Jesus that is nourished by prayer and meditation. Conversion requires us to love other people, especially the outcasts of society. Sometimes conversion requires us to take prophetic stands against evil. The joy found in the new life of Christ overflows in celebrating and supporting all that builds the Reign of God on earth.

✧ Draw up your own "creed" or list of beliefs—the touchstones of your faith. Begin each statement with the phrase, "I believe." Include only beliefs that you are absolutely sure of at this point in your life. Include only what *you* believe.

✧ Pick favorite passages from the Scriptures that have always spoken to you. Read each passage, keeping in mind that the Bible is speaking to you personally and guiding you on your spiritual journey. Then write in your journal why you think each of the passages has been such vital nourishment to your faith.

✧ Draw an image of your hunger for God, the deep longing that you experience for absolute meaning, unconditional love, and joyous hope. Do not worry about the artistic merit of your drawing; simply let the drawing mirror your awareness of this hunger.

✧ Ponder the following questions. (You may want to respond in your journal.)
✦ How do I manifest my faith in daily life? With my family? At work? In the larger community?
✦ Does my faith make me a minister of the Good News, in my own way?

✧ We might not like to think of ourselves as sinners, but as human beings we usually miss the mark of our intentions. We act selfishly, enviously, ungratefully, and even hatefully. To celebrate faith, we need to touch its opposite.

Play a piece of music or sing a song that you find relaxing. Allow yourself to center on God's presence.

Imagine that God's love moves through your heart like a wide, dynamic, pure, cool river. See the banks of this river, dip your hand in the water, and then wade into it.

Now imagine that the flow of the river slows, impeded by floating debris. A logjam traps the swirling, murky water.

Think of the "logjams" or obstacles that build up in your life, the tendencies towards selfishness, greed, isolation, and ingratitude. Feel the darkness and helplessness and dirt when the flow of God's grace no longer runs free.

Turn to Jesus as if he were sitting near you at this moment. Describe your feelings to him. Tell him about the times when you have blocked the flow of God's love. Ask Jesus for help.

Now return to the music, and rest in Christ's love.

✧ Sing a favorite hymn to celebrate your faith.

God's Word

Now that we have been justified by faith, we are at peace with God through . . . Jesus Christ; it is through him, by faith, that we have been admitted into God's favor in which we are living, and look forward exultantly to God's glory. (Romans 5:1–2)

Closing prayer: God's love washes over me like a warm breeze and feeds me when I am cold and sick. God's love is my comfort and my joy. It reaches into the depths of my being and unifies all the aspects of my life. I pray for the gift of faith that is the beginning of all joy.

✧ **Meditation 4** ✧

Solitude

Theme: Merton realized that solitude was essential for monks, and some level of solitude is necessary for all people who seek to be intimate with God. It gives time and space for us to be vulnerable and honest with God and with ourselves.

Opening prayer: O God, lead me into solitude where I can grow in knowledge of you and experience your intimacy in the depths of my heart.

About Merton

At the beginning of his monastic life, Thomas Merton searched out places where he could relish his aloneness:

> My chief joy is to escape to the attic of the garden house and the little broken window that looks out over the valley. There in the silence I love the green grass. The tortured gestures of the apple trees have become part of my prayer. . . . So much do I love this solitude that when I walk out along the road to the old barns that stand alone, far from the new buildings, delight begins to overpower me from head to foot and peace smiles even in the marrow of my bones. (*Sign of Jonas*, [1956], p. 281)

Later in his life, Merton found his desire for more thorough solitude fulfilled when he moved into a cinder block hermitage on a wooded knoll not far from the monastery.

> I went to bed late at the hermitage. All quiet. No lights at Boone's or Newton's. Cold. Lay in bed realizing what I was: I was *happy!* . . .
>
> No matter what anyone else might do or say about it, however they might judge or evaluate it, all is irrelevant to the reality of my vocation to solitude even though I am not a typical hermit. Quite the contrary, perhaps. (*Vow of Conversation*, p. 112)

Even though he was happy in the hermitage, Merton realized that he could not entertain any illusions. Solitude stripped away all pretense about himself. His solitude even allowed him to confront his own death. At one point, he felt death pass him in the darkness:

> How often in the last years I have thought of death. It has been present to me and I have "understood" and known that I must die. Yet last night, only for a moment, in passing and so to speak without grimness or drama, I momentarily experienced the fact that I, this body, this self, will simply not exist. A flash of the "not-thereness" of being dead. Without fear or grief, without anything. Just *not there*. And this, I suppose, is one of the first tastes of the fruits of solitude. (*Vow of Conversation*, p. 108)

Pause: Ponder your own desire for solitude, your hunger to center entirely on intimacy with God.

Merton's Words

The solitary life makes sense only when it is centered entirely on the love of God. Without this, everything is triviality. Love of God in Himself, for Himself, sought only in His will in total surrender. Anything but this in solitude is nausea and absurdity. (*Vow of Conversation*, p. 155)

Reflection

To think of solitude in idealistic images is tempting, but Merton knew that the real joy of a solitary life is not limited to an appreciation of the beauty of nature or even a feeling of peace in one's heart. It involves answering a call at the center of the heart, a call to listen to the voice of God, to hear and pray, not later, but now.

Merton taught that solitude allows no room for self-preoccupation. Solitude invites us to forget ourselves in the presence of God and to sacrifice our hidden agendas for God's. The illusion that we can exist separately from God is shattered, so that we can move toward the humility, emptiness, and purity preserved by the nurturing of God's love.

Solitude invites us to stay with the feeling of inner emptiness—not escape it through distraction or words—but sink within it, allowing it to be transformed as God wills. In our loneliness, according to Merton, we discover that God longs to be alone in us. Union with God—this is the reason we need to be faithful to solitude.

Rather than destroying our relationships with other people, solitude nurtures love and solidarity. Merton remarks:

> The solitary is one who is aware of solitude in himself as a basic and inevitable human reality, not just as something which affects him as an isolated individual. Hence his solitude is the foundation of a deep, pure and gentle sympathy with all other men. (*Disputed Questions*, pp. 188–189)

Above all, solitude means little unless it is centered entirely on the love of God. With this love, solitude enriches every aspect of a person's existence.

✧ Take a walk in the woods, in a park, down your street, or in some environment that appeals to you, and just be present to God's gifts. If you cannot go out, sit at a window with a view, and just be present to the God who is with you.

✧ List people in your life with whom you have a meaningful relationship. When you are finished, repeat each name slowly. Let your heart extend to that person with compassion.

Then ponder this question: Could any of these relationships be further enriched if I spent more time in solitary prayer and reflection?

✧ Make a list of distractions, habits, illusions, or cultural messages that block your hunger for solitude. Read over the list and ponder the ways that you may have ignored your call to solitude. Consider and make an action plan for how you can make some space, and also time, for solitude in your life.

✧ This guided imagery may help you touch some memories of the consolations of solitude:

Imagine yourself as a child. . . . You enter a dark room that feels welcoming and warm. . . . You close the door behind you to protect your secret experience. . . . Standing in the room for a while, you become aware that a loving, dark warmth radiates from the center of the room. . . . You draw close and curl up next to it, trusting in the silence and the darkness. . . . Now take time to remain in silence and peace near the secret warmth, the love of God, in the depths of your being.

✧ One of the fruits of solitude is gratitude. Pray a litany of names of people you love, and after each name, express your gratitude by thanking God for the gift of that person in your life. In the same fashion, pray a litany of thanks for all the other gifts in your life.

God's Word

"And when you pray, do not imitate the hypocrites: they love to say their prayers standing up in the synagogues and at the street corners for people to see them. In truth I tell you, they have had their reward. But when you pray, go to your private room, shut yourself in, and so pray to your [God] who is in that secret place, and your [God] who sees all that is done in secret will reward you." (Matthew 6:5–6)

In those days [Jesus] went onto the mountain to pray; and he spent the whole night in prayer to God. When day came he summoned his disciples and picked out twelve of them; he called them apostles. (Luke 6:12–13)

Closing prayer: God, in times of solitude, teach me gentleness and compassion and show me how to cultivate a pure love in the depths of my heart. Help me open the doorway of solitude into the mystery of your presence and the power of your love.

In Silence

Theme: Growth in spiritual maturity requires external silence, which deepens the silence within and leads to more profound union with Christ.

Opening prayer: Let me learn to live in silence, God of mystery. Immerse my anxieties, tensions, words, and gestures in silence and anchor my life in the silence of your love.

About Merton

Merton's attraction to silence remained consistent throughout his life. As a young monk, he basked in the silence of the woods around the monastery:

> "This afternoon I was content looking at the low green rampart of woods that divides us from the rest of the universe and listening to the deep silence: content not for the sake of the scene or the silence but because of God." (*Sign of Jonas* [1956], p. 69)

Later, alone in the hermitage, he wrote in his journal: "I can imagine no other joy on earth than to have such a place to be at peace in. To live in silence, to think and write, to listen to the wind and to all the voices of the wood" (*Vow of Conversation*, p. 152).

This poetic description hints at the unique call to solitude and silence that Merton enjoyed:

> To deliver oneself up, to hand oneself over, entrust oneself completely to the silence of a wide landscape of woods and hills, or sea, or desert; to sit still while the sun comes up over that land and fills its silences with light. To pray and work in the morning and to labor and rest in the afternoon, and to sit still again in meditation in the evening when night falls upon that land and when the silence fills itself with darkness and with stars. This is a true and special vocation. There are few who are willing to belong completely to such silence, to let it soak into their bones, to breathe nothing but silence, to feed on silence, and to turn the very substance of their life into a living and vigilant silence. (*Thoughts in Solitude*, p. 97)

In his hermitage, silence filled Merton's heart with hope even during periods of doubt:

> There was heavy rain all night. Now the rain on the roof accentuates the silence and surrounds the dryness and light of the hermitage as though with love and peace. The liberty and tranquillity of this place are indescribable, more than any bodily peace. This is a gift of God marked with His simplicity and His purity. How one's heart opens and what hope arises in the core of my being! (*Vow of Conversation*, p. 113)

Pause: Reflect on this question: When have I enjoyed silence in my life?

Merton's Words

There is in all visible things an invisible fecundity, a dimmed light, a meek namelessness, a hidden wholeness. This mysterious Unity and Integrity is Wisdom, the Mother of all, *Natura naturans*. There is in all things an inexhaustible sweetness and purity, a silence that is a fount of action and joy. It rises up in wordless gentleness and flows out to me from the unseen roots of all created being, welcoming me tenderly, saluting me with indescribable humility. This is at once my own being, my own nature, and the Gift of my Creator's Thought and Art within me, speaking as Hagia Sophia, speaking as my sister, Wisdom. ("Hagia Sophia," *The Collected Poems of Thomas Merton*, p. 363)

My life is a listening, His [God's] is a speaking. My salvation is to hear and respond. For this, my life must be silent. . . . If our life is poured out in useless words, we will never hear anything, will never become anything. (*Thoughts in Solitude*, pp. 72, 88)

When your tongue is silent, you can rest in the silence of the forest. When your imagination is silent, the forest speaks to you, tells you of its unreality and of the Reality of God. But when your mind is silent, then the forest suddenly becomes magnificently real and blazes transparently with the Reality of God. . . . This is prayer, and this is glory! (*Sign of Jonas* [1956], p. 332)

Reflection

Merton drew a distinction between outer and inner silence. He thought of outer silence as the absence of sound, the quiet time he needed to read, meditate, study, and simply not talk to anybody. He realized the need for external silence in a world so given to noise.

But Merton's quest for silence led beyond the mere absence of sound. Outward silence opens the door to inner silence; inner silence is the silence of the "true" or authentic self before God. In its deepest form, this inner silence dispenses with thoughts and words, and we are simply present, listening, attending to God and our true self: "My knowledge of myself in silence (not by reflection on my self, but by penetration to the mystery of my true self which is beyond words and concepts) . . . opens out into the silence and the 'subjectivity' of God's own self" (*Thoughts in Solitude*, p. 68). A person who longs for the silence of God will find that the word is received in the soul's deep silence. Receiving the word then becomes a silent union with God.

Besides union with God, inner silence permits encounter with the innermost, true self that is obscure, hidden, veiled: "There is a silent self within us whose presence is disturbing precisely because it is so silent: it *can't* be spoken. It has to remain silent. To articulate it, to verbalize it, is to tamper with it, and in some ways to destroy it" (Thomas Merton, *Love and Living*, p. 40). Inner stillness, inner silence is complete presence to God and to ourself.

To reach this point of inner silence demands external quiet, an openness of heart, an emptying of the mind or letting go of stray thoughts and preoccupations. Finally, inner silence is a gift God gives when we are ready to listen and attend.

✧ Reread "Merton's Words" slowly. If a particular line strikes you, stay with it. Let God speak to your heart through these words of Merton.

✧ Slowly read this prayer by Merton: "Let me seek, then, the gift of silence, . . . where everything I touch is turned into prayer: where the sky is my prayer, the birds are my prayer, the wind in the trees is my prayer, for God is all in all" (*Thoughts in Solitude*, p. 91).

✧ Here is one way of opening yourself to inner silence. Recall God's presence; sit quietly with that thought. Then relax your whole body by stretching your feet, then your legs, and so on, up to your face. For some time, be conscious of your breathing. Breathe slowly and deeply for a while. Let your whole body relax. Next, begin focusing on a prayer word—for example, *silence* or *wisdom*. Silently repeat the word as you slowly inhale and then as you exhale. Pray the word in harmony with your breathing. At some point, and only you can know when, cease praying the word. Rest in the silence, attending and listening for whatever God tells you. If a distracting thought rumbles into your mind, patiently repeat the prayer word again until the stray thought leaves. Dwell in the silence.

Throughout the day in any spare moments, attend to God in this way.

✧ Silence in mind and heart teaches us to listen and attend to the people in our life also. Recall the conversations you have had today, as many as you can. Then determine which conversations caused confusion and a sense of emptiness. Could these conversations have been more constructive if you had listened more or been more silent? Were the fruitful conversations the product of your ability to silently attend to the other person?

✧ Write a prayer that expresses your own desire for Christ's silence within, your need to communicate with Christ without words or without thinking. After writing the prayer, read it, and let it invite you to rest in God's silence.

God's Word

For God alone my soul waits in silence,
for my hope comes from God.

(Adapted from Psalm 62:5)

Closing prayer: Thank you for the invitation to silence, O my God. Your silence reveals the depths of my soul. May silence with you nourish my heart and permeate all my relationships. Into the silence of my soul, send your holy wisdom.

Prayer of the Heart

Theme: Prayer, an essential part of each person's life, demands attention to an authentic self as well as interior silence and discipline.

Opening prayer: My God, you have given me a desire for prayer. Teach me how to seek you in the depths of my being and recognize you as the deepest imperative of my life.

About Merton

At the time of his baptism and first Communion, Thomas Merton acknowledged the strongest pull in his life:

> And God, that center Who is everywhere, and whose circumference is nowhere, finding me, through incorporation with Christ, incorporated into this immense and tremendous gravitational movement which is love, which is the Holy Spirit, loved me. (*Seven Storey Mountain*, p. 225)

Answering this gravitational force in his life brought Merton to the monastery doors. As a Trappist monk, he learned the traditional monastic practices of meditation and contemplation and participated in a full liturgical life: the sacraments, psalmody, Gregorian chant, and the meditative reading of the Scriptures. These methods of praying complemented his personal prayer.

Merton did not describe his personal way of praying to any extent, but in a letter to Abdul Aziz he described his "prayer of the heart," or what is commonly referred to today as centering prayer:

> Strictly speaking I have a very simple way of prayer. It is centered entirely on attention to the presence of God and to His will and His love. That is to say that it is centered on *faith* by which alone we can know the presence of God. One might say this gives my meditation the character described by the Prophet as "being before God as if you saw Him." Yet it does not mean imagining anything or conceiving a precise image of God, for to my mind this would be a kind of idolatry. On the contrary, it is a matter of adoring Him as invisible and infinitely beyond our comprehension. . . . There is in my heart this great thirst to recognize totally the nothingness of all that is not God. My prayer is then a kind of praise rising up out of the center of Nothing and Silence. (Shannon, ed., *Hidden Ground of Love*, pp. 63–64)

Prayer such as this unveils God in all reality, God in the everyday-ness of life, in the body, in nature, and in people. Merton saw all occasions as times of prayer: "Walking down a street, sweeping a floor, washing dishes, hoeing beans, reading a book, taking a stroll in the woods—all can be enriched with contemplation and with the obscure sense of the presence of God" (Cunningham, ed., *Spiritual Master*, p. 352).

Pause: Relax, breathe slowly, rhythmically, and rest silently in God's loving presence. Gently let go of thoughts and distractions.

Merton's Words

Contemplative prayer is a deep and simplified spiritual activity in which the mind and will rest in a unified and simple concentration upon God, turned to Him, intent upon Him and absorbed in His own light, with a simple gaze which is perfect adoration because it silently tells

God that we have left everything else and desire even to leave our own selves for His sake, and that He alone is important to us, He alone is our desire and our life, and nothing else can give us any joy. (*New Seeds of Contemplation*, p. 243)

Reflection

Merton recognized that to pray meant to discover God as the source of one's being: "By 'prayer of the heart' we seek God himself present in the depths of our being and meet him there by invoking the name of Jesus in faith, wonder, and love" (*Contemplative Prayer*, pp. 30–31).

Merton encouraged meditation on the truths of salvation history not only as a way to deepen our faith and understanding but as leading toward a loving intuition of the truth. All forms of prayer, he said, should end in love. Meditation may begin as an intellectual activity that recollects the person before God, but "most of all it aims at bringing you to a state of almost constant loving attention to God, and dependence on Him" (*New Seeds of Contemplation*, p. 217).

"Prayer of the heart," or contemplative prayer, may use few words or none, but it requires our faith and a willing heart. Trust, joy, loving attentiveness, expectation—not a particular prayer technique—become important. Merton explained that this prayer "begins not so much with 'considerations' as with a 'return to the heart,' finding one's deepest center, awakening the profound depths of our being in the presence of God who is the source of our being and our life" (*Contemplative Prayer*, p. 30). Merton taught that simply "walking with God" was one of the surest ways of perpetuating a life of prayer.

Contemplation reorients our life on God and reminds us of our need for ongoing conversion and divine mercy. Prayer of the heart grows out of the quality of one's life as a whole and immeasurably nourishes one's life in return.

✧ One of the biggest difficulties in prayer is the inability to relax. Begin by calming your body, taking time to concentrate on each part. Now become aware of your breathing. Do not concentrate too hard or attempt to control your breathing. Simply give attention to the air as it passes through your nostrils; be aware of it. If you become distracted, gently return your attention to your breathing.

This exercise will not only relax you but it will also increase your awareness of yourself. You may want to think of each breath as the breath of God moving through you.

✧ Read "Merton's Words" again and take time to rest in your own desire for God's love. Use a mantra (a word or phrase that has spiritual importance for you, such as *love, Jesus, Jesus have mercy, God of love*) to ward off distractions. Simply remain in the presence of God.

✧ Awareness of the need for prayer rises out of life events, especially those that involve suffering or conflict. Describe one or two events in your life that have opened your heart to deeper prayer. How were you more sensitive to God's call during this time in your life? What type of prayer became important to you?

✧ Merton suggested that contemplative prayer can begin with reading the Scriptures or gazing at a crucifix or a favorite landscape. Read the Scriptures, gaze at a crucifix, pray in your church, or go for a walk. Be present to where you are. If some passage that you read or something that you see absorbs your attention, let it gradually bring you to rest in God. When you become distracted, return to your original focus.

✧ You may be asking yourself whether you are being drawn toward contemplative prayer. Answer the following questions based on some of Merton's advice about when to let go of meditation and rest in God's love. (See *New Seeds of Contemplation*, pp. 240–242)
+ Do you find that your ordinary ways of praying are urging you to give yourself more fully and generously to God?
+ Do you find peace simply resting in God?
+ Do you find yourself more sensitive to your sinfulness and a need for God's mercy?

✦ Do you feel that the normal interests of daily life will never satisfy your desire for more love and that you will only find satisfaction in the depths of this starkly simple prayer?

Answering these questions may indicate a deeper need to share in the very life of God. You may uncover the need to include the contemplative dimension of prayer in your life.

God's Word

Upon my bed at night
I sought him whom my soul loves;
I sought him, but found him not;
I called him, but he gave no answer.
"I will rise now and go about the city,
    in the streets and in the squares;
I will seek him whom my soul loves."

(Song of Songs 3:1–2, NRSV)

Closing prayer: Dear God, make my prayer one of silence, humility, and purity of heart so that my inner life can become a revelation of your presence.

✧ **Meditation 7** ✧

Wandering
in the Wilderness

Theme: Our spiritual journey inevitably leads into a wilderness of the heart, a desolate, purifying place where we learn to let go of false hopes and illusions. Merton urges us to be patient and put our humble trust in God.

Opening prayer: Loving God, teach me to remain still, to trust in you, to listen to your call in my desert times. Let me learn the meaning of complete and constant dependence on you alone.

About Merton

When he first entered the monastery, Thomas Merton viewed monastic life through rose-colored glasses, but he also acknowledged the transforming effect that the monastic tradition would have on his spirit: "The beginning of love is truth, and before He will give us His love, God must cleanse our souls of the lies that are in them" (*Seven Storey Mountain*, p. 372).

During his novitiate, Merton had his physical and spiritual stamina tested. In accord with the vision of Saint Benedict, monasticism provides a path of sacrifice, a narrow way into the wilderness where the soul is stripped of pretense and prepared to receive God. Merton experienced the longing that drove generations of men and women into the wilderness, away from the allurements of secular society toward the place of purification necessary for union with God in love.

The sacrifices, labors, and routine of Trappist life prodded Merton to leave his former life and embark on his spiritual journey. The schedule was grueling. He rose at 2 a.m. for prayer and meditation that would last for two hours. All day he worked, studied, prayed, and meditated. His meals consisted chiefly of vegetables and bread, and he added his own personal forms of asceticism. When he wrote lyrically about the countryside surrounding Gethsemani, he too often overlooked Kentucky weather: the muggy heat of summer and the damp cold of winter. Working in the fields encouraged contemplation, but it often proved exhausting.

Monastic discipline gave order to Merton's fragmented life. Indeed, the discipline and regularity of monastic life has one purpose: to cultivate the monk's inner wilderness for the sake of a more sensitive awareness of God's love. In the epilogue of *Seven Storey Mountain*, Merton hears God addressing him:

> I will give you what you desire. I will lead you into solitude. I will lead you by the way that you cannot possibly understand, because I want it to be the quickest way.
>
> Therefore all the things around you will be armed against you, to deny you, to hurt you, to give you pain, and therefore to reduce you to solitude.
>
> . . . You will have gifts, and they will break you with their burden. You will have pleasures of prayer, and they will sicken you and you will fly from them.
>
> . . . But you shall taste the true solitude of my anguish and my poverty and I shall lead you into the high places of my joy and you shall die in Me and find all things in My mercy which has created you for this end.
>
> . . .
>
> That you may become the brother of God and learn to know the Christ of the burnt men. (Pp. 422–423)

Pause: What wilderness are you experiencing in your heart at this time in your life? How is it asking you to depend on God alone?

Merton's Words

Let us never forget that the ordinary way to contemplation lies through a desert without trees and without beauty and without water. The spirit enters a wilderness and travels blindly in directions that seem to lead away from vision, away from God, away from all fulfillment and joy. It may become almost impossible to believe that this road goes anywhere at all except to a desolation full of dry bones—the ruin of all our hopes and good intentions. (*New Seeds of Contemplation*, p. 235)

The Desert Father could not afford to be an illuminist [one who seeks visions]. He could not dare risk attachment to his own ego, or the dangerous ecstasy of self-will. He could not retain the slightest identification with his superficial, transient, self-constructed self. He had to lose himself in the inner, hidden reality of a self that was transcendent, mysterious, half-known, and lost in Christ. He had to die to the values of transient existence as Christ had died to them on the Cross, and rise from the dead with Him in the light of an entirely new wisdom. (*The Wisdom of the Desert*, p. 7)

Reflection

The wilderness, or desert, formed the backdrop for the prophets, the Psalms, and the Exodus. John the Baptist preached in the wilderness, and the Spirit drove Jesus into the desert to be tempted. The call for each of us, according to Merton, is to recover new life after being purified and tested like Christ in the wilderness. Specifically, Merton believed that God calls a monk into the desert where his only sustenance can be Jesus.

The wilderness, that is, the times of suffering, anxiety, helplessness, and loss, strips us of our usual props. Social respectability loses some of its allure, and our usual consolations fail to satisfy. The Spirit urges us to seek time alone with God. Even though we may fight these promptings, solitude attracts us. We are drawn toward the wilderness, into the experience of suffering, anxiety, helplessness, or loss—wherever our desert lies.

Our desert and wilderness can be a meaningless job, chronic illness, a crumbling relationship, or the loss of a loved one. Whatever wilderness we travel into, God is ever inviting us to depend on the love poured out in Jesus. About the Israelites in the desert, Merton concluded: "God's plan was that they [the Chosen People] should learn to love Him in the wilderness and that they should always look back upon the time in the desert as the idyllic time of their life with Him alone" (*Thoughts in Solitude*, p. 20).

In the midst of the desert, we might grumble and rebel like the people of Israel. We might temporarily abandon the God who truly liberates us from our slavery, the God who loves us totally. God understands this rebellion and anger as our attempt to control our own destiny, to call all the shots. God trusts that once we have faced the desert, confronted the reality of our vulnerability, we will rush into the divine embrace.

✧ Meditate on these two statements from the section "About Merton." Imagine that Jesus is addressing the words to you. Then ponder how the words apply to your life; let yourself remember your own wilderness.

✦ "All the things around you will be armed against you, to deny you, to hurt you, to give you pain, and therefore to reduce you to solitude."

✦ "You will have gifts, and they will break you with their burden."

Finally, ask yourself: How did these wilderness experiences draw me closer to God?

✧ Write a description of one of the wildernesses in which you are wandering right now: Who and what is involved? What do you feel? How did you wander into the wilderness? Why are you there?

When you have finished writing the description, reflect on these questions:

✦ Have you grumbled at and rebelled against the wilderness?

✦ Have you tried to distract yourself from the wilderness by such things as overeating, staying ultra-busy, watching hours of television?

✦ Have you tried to deny that you are in a desert?

✦ Does part of you really want to see things as they really are?

✦ Would you be better off if, like the Israelites, you got on with the march through your desert, recognizing that it is a desert and that you can get through it with God's help?

Talk with God about your desert experience, and ask for the graces that you need to march through it.

✧ The wilderness is often prosaic, the mundane experience of life.

✦ How has routine become a desert for me?

✦ Do I have any romantic illusions about the spiritual life? What are these? Have they kept me from experiencing the deeper call of God's love?

✦ Am I looking for a good feeling from prayer or from religious experience? Ask God for strength to rely on faith alone.

✧ After a period of stretching, calm breathing, and centering, enter into this guided meditation:

Imagine a desert . . . the wide horizon, oceans of sand, heat, strong wind. . . . Feel the dryness and desolation of this vast, empty space. . . . Recall a time in your life that felt like this. . . . Describe the time to yourself and let the desolation sink in, the feelings of loneliness and emptiness, of traveling without hope. . . .

Now imagine a desert transformed by a rain. . . . Flowers spring up everywhere. . . . Dry sand becomes a lush garden. . . . Recall the graces that have fertilized your soul during your desert times . . . the people and events that helped you through your desolation . . . the gifts of warmth, food, and rest. . . . Let a prayer of hope and thanksgiving rise in your heart. . . . Ask God for the strength to trust, to remain patiently and humbly in the desert, waiting for a sign of the Promised Land.

God's Word

Filled with the Holy Spirit, Jesus left the Jordan and was led by the Spirit into the desert, for forty days being put to the test by the devil. During that time he ate nothing and at the end he was hungry. Then the devil said to him, "If you are Son of God, tell this stone to turn into a loaf." But Jesus replied, "Scripture says: [People] live not on bread alone." (Luke 4:1–4)

Closing prayer: "Therefore, I will now allure her," says Yahweh, alluding to Israel, "and bring her into the wilderness, and speak tenderly to her" (Hosea 2:14). O God, no one wants to spend a lot of time in a desert, but when life leads me into the wilderness and strips me of all my resources, please let me know that I can count on your love.

✦ Meditation 8 ✦

Sharing Our Talents

Theme: Merton realized that people must use their unique gifts for the good of humankind and in praise of a generous Creator. Merton's special gift was writing; it provided a way to strengthen his relationship with God and to companion others on their spiritual journey.

Opening prayer: God of creation, give me the wisdom and courage to express my faith, hope, and love through the unique talents that you have given me.

About Merton

Thomas Merton knew he wanted to be a writer. He wrote fiction and poems before he joined the Trappists, and those works record his religious development and reveal a person whose spiritual journey was intimately connected with his desire to be a writer.

While teaching at Saint Bonaventure College, Merton pondered whether he should work at the Friendship House in Harlem or enter the monastery. In a journal he kept at the time, he expressed a desire to transform his life completely, even if he had to sacrifice writing. The conflict between writing and complete dedication to the spiritual life continued through his early years as a Trappist.

When his superiors learned about his interest in writing, they encouraged Merton to pursue his talent and asked him to write about the lives of several Cistercians. Then, with the approval of his superiors, Merton took a step that would strip away his anonymity. He wrote his autobiography, *The Seven Storey Mountain*, which was published under his own name.

To everyone's surprise, Merton's story made him a national celebrity. But even while he was writing *The Seven Storey Mountain*, he anticipated the conflict between his hidden and public lives: "Sometimes I am mortally afraid. There are days when there seems to be nothing left of my vocation—my contemplative vocation—but a few ashes. And everybody calmly tells me: 'Writing is your vocation'" (*Seven Storey Mountain*, p 410).

Despite his doubts, Merton set to work on a new book, *Seeds of Contemplation*, but he felt caught in a paradox. He was writing about losing himself in God, but in order to do so he had to speak from the very self he wanted to sacrifice. Around the time of his ordination, he lamented, "since I became a great success in the book business I have been becoming more and more of a failure in my vocation" (*Sign of Jonas* [1953], p. 210).

After collapsing from exhaustion soon after his ordination, Merton emerged from his illness with a new sense of himself and his call. He fully embraced his identity as monk and writer since each of us are, as he said, "called to share with God the work of *creating* the truth of our identity" (*New Seeds of Contemplation*, p. 32). The truth of Merton's identity was that God had given him the gift of writing.

Because it heightened Merton's spiritual awareness, the act of writing brought him more quickly to a point of transformation in his life. He realized that losing the self resulted not in self-alienation, but self-discovery: "If I am to be a saint . . . it seems that I must get there by writing books in a Trappist monastery" (*Sign of Jonas* [1953], p. 233).

Pause: Reflect on a talent you possess that has heightened your awareness of your spiritual life. How has the development or lack of development of your talent influenced your relationship with others and with God?

Merton's Words

I have tried to learn in my writing a monastic lesson I could probably not have learned otherwise: to let go of my idea of myself, to take myself with more than one grain of salt. If the monastic life is a life of hardship and sacrifice, I would say that for me most of the hardship has come in connection with writing. It is possible to doubt whether I have become a monk (a doubt I have to live with), but it is not possible to doubt that I am a writer, that I was born one and will most probably die as one. Disconcerting, disedifying as it is, this seems to be my lot and my vocation. It is what God has given me in order that I might give it back to Him.

In religious terms, this is simply a matter of accepting life, and everything in life as a gift, and clinging to none of it, as far as you are able. You give some of it to others, if you can. . . .

All life tends to grow like this, in mystery inscaped with paradox and contradiction, yet centered, in its very heart, on the divine mercy. (McDonnell, ed., *A Thomas Merton Reader*, pp. 16–17)

Reflection

In Merton's struggle to integrate the gift of writing with his call to the life of a monk, he concluded that in order to be true to his God-given gift he had to write. He had to share God's gift for the good of other people. God calls all people first to identify their talents and skills and then to use them to build the Reign of God.

In his writings, Merton allows readers to go on his spiritual journey with him. His quest for Christ is opened to us. While our way of sharing our journey to Christ may be different, the call to share the journey is the same for every Christian. Some of us may be teachers, some dancers, some engineers, some salespeople, some mechanics, but each of us can be Christ for others by doing what Merton did through writing: "[Merton] tells us about himself, and we see ourselves as in a mirror and not only ourselves, but every person" (William H. Shannon, *Silent Lamp*, p. 6).

Even though few of us are called to be writers, many of the forms of writing that Merton used can assist us in our spiritual journey. Merton wrote in journals to record his thoughts and feelings and to use as resource material that he edited for publication. About journal writing, Merton commented: "Keeping a journal has taught me that there is not so much new in your life as you sometimes think. . . . Still, it is true that one penetrates deeper and deeper into the same ideas and the same experiences" (*Sign of Jonas* [1953], p. 204).

Another form of self-expression that Merton used was letters. During his life, he conducted a prodigious correspondence. Merton's letters (over four thousand) are spontaneous manifestations of his spiritual wisdom and social concern, along with doses of his wit.

Merton wrote poetry that reflected his spiritual journey as well as his empathy for the lives of other people. In his poems, Merton could also laugh at aspects of community life, but always with respect toward other people.

Merton wrote, and we should consider ways to articulate our own spiritual journey, the story of our own turning toward God.

✧ To paraphrase Merton, "What gifts, talents, and skills has God given you in order that you might give them back to God and your sisters and brothers?" Compose a list of all of them. Include skills that you have learned, gifts of personality (for example, being a good listener, having a rich sense of humor), and talents that God has given you, but you have developed.

After you have done a thorough inventory, thank God for each gift.

✧ Select a talent that you are ignoring. Can you make time on a regular basis to develop this talent?

✧ Merton remarked: "If I am to be a saint . . . it seems that I must get there by writing books in a Trappist monastery." Examine your own life, and then complete this sentence for yourself: "If I am to be a saint, it seems that I must get there by . . ." In completing the sentence, be sure to include how your work, family, community, and other interests will fit into the "getting there."

✧ Begin a journal that explores your own spiritual journey. Consider including a daily log of significant thoughts, prayers, or questions; a list of books and poems you have read; drawings; imaginary dialogs with other people, Jesus, or your body; and issues you are trying to work through. In journal writing we often find out what we did not know we knew.

✧ Draw the path or life-line (graph) of your spiritual journey, marking all your major turning points.
✦ Choose one of these turning points and describe it in your journal. Write for thirty minutes or more.
✦ At the end, reread your description. What could God be telling you through this event in your life?

✧ Write a letter to a person who has touched your life on a spiritual level. Thank that person for the gifts he or she has offered you.

God's Word

The man who had received the five talents came forward bringing five more. "Sir," he said, "you entrusted me with five talents; here are five more that I have made." His master said to him, "Well done, good and trustworthy servant; you have shown you are trustworthy in small things; I will trust you with greater; come and join in your master's happiness." (Matthew 25:20–21)

Closing prayer: O God, let my life become a story of grace, a poem addressed to you. Give me the courage to use my talents in order to understand my ongoing conversion and to serve the needs of other people.

Natural Contemplation

Theme: For those who are prepared, receptive, and open to love, God is experienced at the heart of the created world.

Opening prayer: Thank you, O Creator, for the many wonders in our universe, for all the sparks of creation that rise up and greet my eyes and evoke my love for you.

About Merton

Thomas Merton reveled in the Kentucky landscape of knolls and forests that surrounded the monastery complex. "I looked at all this in great tranquillity, with my soul and spirit quiet. For me landscape seems to be important for contemplation; anyway, I have no scruples about loving it" (*Sign of Jonas* [1956], p. 113).

Merton's sacramental vision made him more and more aware of the seasons as complementary to the liturgy and to the process of death and resurrection in his own spiritual life.

The first Sunday of Lent, as I now know, is a great feast. Christ has sanctified the desert and in the desert I discovered it. The woods have all become young in the discipline of spring: but it is the discipline of expectancy only. . . . There are no buds. Buds are not guessed at or thought of, this early in Lent. But the wilderness shines with promise. The land is dressed in simplicity and strength. Everything foretells the coming of the holy spring. I had never before spoken so freely or so intimately with woods, hills, birds, water, and sky. (*Sign of Jonas* [1956], p. 273)

From the perspective of his hermitage, Merton wrote: "One thing the hermitage is making me see is that the universe is my home and I am nothing if not part of it" (*Vow of Conversation*, p. 156). With even increasing sensitivity, he noticed the natural dramas that unfolded around him each day.

In the afternoon, there were lots of pretty little myrtle warblers playing and diving for insects in the low pine branches over my head. So close, I could almost touch them. I was awed at their loveliness, their quick flight, their lookings and chirpings, the yellow spot on the back revealed in flight. A sense of total kinship with them as if they and I were all of the same nature and as if that nature were nothing but love. (*Vow of Conversation*, p. 95)

In the last chapter of *New Seeds of Contemplation*, Merton images the world as a garden, as a temple, as a paradise where God dances. God dances in and through creation and all participate in the rhythm. This universal dance originates in the redeeming love of Jesus Christ through the power of the Spirit.

The Lord plays and diverts Himself in the garden of His creation, and if we could let go of our own obsession with what we think is the meaning of it all, we might be able to hear His call and follow Him in His mysterious, cosmic dance. . . .

For the world and time are the dance of the Lord in emptiness. The silence of the spheres is the music of a wedding feast. The more we persist in misunderstanding the phenomena of life, the more we analyze them out into strange finalities and complex purposes of our own, the more we involve ourselves in sadness, absurdity and despair. . . .

Yet the fact remains that we are invited to forget ourselves on purpose, cast our awful solemnity to the winds and join in the general dance. (Pp. 296–297)

Pause: Reflect on your own vision of the natural world. Do you feel separate from creation, or do you feel part of the dance?

Merton's Words

The contemplation of God in nature, which the Greek Fathers called *theoria physica* [natural contemplation], has both a positive and a negative aspect. On the one hand, *theoria physica* is a positive recognition of God as He is manifested in the essences (*logoi*) of all things. It is not a speculative science of nature but rather a habit of religious awareness which endows the soul with a kind of intuitive perception of God as He is reflected in His creation. This instinctive religious view of things is not acquired by study so much as by ascetic detachment. . . . The negative aspect of *theoria physica* is an equally instinctive realization of the vanity and illusion of all things as soon as they are considered apart from their right order and reference to God their Creator. (McDonnell, ed., *A Thomas Merton Reader*, p. 384)

You flowers and trees, you hills and streams, you fields, flocks and wild birds, you books, you poems, and you people, I am unutterably alone in the midst of you. The irrational hunger that sometimes gets into the depths of my will, tries to swing my deepest self away from God and direct it to your love. I try to touch you with the deep fire that is in the center of my heart, but I cannot touch you without defiling both you and myself, and I am abashed, solitary and helpless, surrounded by a beauty that can never belong to me.

But this sadness generates within me an unspeakable reverence for the holiness of created things, for they are pure and perfect and they belong to God and they are mirrors of His beauty. He is mirrored in all things like sunlight in clean water: but if I try to drink the light that is in the water I only shatter the reflection. (*Sign of Jonas* [1956], pp. 232–233)

Reflection

Merton borrowed the concept of "natural contemplation" from the Greek Fathers, translating the phrase to mean that we can have a true appreciation of nature and an awareness of God's presence in all of creation. Natural contemplation is possible if we strive for purity or openness of heart.

Merton teaches that as we learn to love God and to express our gratitude for the gifts that we receive, we purify and further open our heart to God present in creation. In other words, unless we attend to God's presence within us, we will not be able to see the holiness around us.

Once we see the world with a pure and open heart, we also transfigure it. We no longer see the world as only physical reality but as a revelation of love. As a result, natural contemplation deepens our respect for the cosmos.

By opening our eyes to the revelation of God in creation, we cease trying to impose our will on creation. We seek harmony with the universe rather than domination. We approach creation as holy ground, sacred space. Merton calls us to relate intimately and reverently to the natural world and to participate in the dance of creation.

✧ Merton used the camera as a tool for contemplating nature. The aperture of the camera was the opening to his heart. He tried to see objects in nature in a way that allowed them to reveal their hidden dimension, their silent mysterious depth.

Choose any camera and load it with film; take extra film with you. Then go to a place in nature that seems to hold some mystery for you. It does not have to be a place of obvious or dramatic beauty.

Walk around the landscape, using the camera whenever you want to concentrate on an object or scene. Allow the image in the camera's viewfinder to imprint itself on your open heart. Then take a picture.

The purpose in using the camera is not art but prayer, so do not become frustrated if the pictures are not "beautiful." The camera is a tool that allows you to develop a contemplative way of seeing. Choose one or two of your images and put them in a place where they can remind you of your heart's desire to see God's love in the world.

✧ Walk, swim, bicycle, jog, canoe, or cross-country ski (for those in northern winter's grip). When you are out in the natural world, pray these words of Merton's in harmony with your strides, breath, pedaling, or paddling: "God is reflected in creation."

✧ Merton writes: "I exist under trees. I walk in the woods out of necessity" (Thomas Merton, *Day of a Stranger*, p. 432). What landscape draws you toward God? Write a prose-poem that describes your relationship with the shore, the woods, the desert, the mountains, and so on.

✧ Reread "Merton's Words" and write a prayer of gratitude, expressing your appreciation of the world around you. Be as specific as you can in your description.

✧ Create a sacred gesture toward creation, such as a bow or a dance. The gesture should reflect your response to God in the world around you. Repeat the gesture slowly and attentively for a short time.
Close this ritual experience with a short prayer, for example, I gratefully "join in the general dance."

God's Word

The world and all that is in it belong to Yahweh,
the earth and all who live on it.
Yahweh built it on the deep waters,
laid its foundations in the oceans' depths.
Who has the right to climb Yahweh's mountain?
Or stand in this holy place?
Those who are pure in act and in thought,
who do not worship idols
or make false promises.
(Psalm 24:1–4)

Closing prayer: O God, I lift up my heart to you. Awaken me to spring breezes, flowers, clouds, and winter's frost as messages from you. Lure me toward you with day and night, spring and fall, reptile and mammal—everything. Plant seeds of hope in my heart so that I can dance with joy toward the eternal sun.

✧ Meditation 10 ✧

The Call to Service

Theme: All Christians, even contemplative monks, are called to reshape the world, become socially involved in building a new creation, and share with others the silence and peace found in a life centered on Christ.

Opening prayer: O God of compassion, give me the strength to avoid the frantic activity and busyness that alienate me from myself and weaken my ability to love others. Just as Jesus served his neighbor, may I do likewise.

About Merton

Once in the monastery, Thomas Merton no longer needed to judge the outside world but was free to relate to it in a more positive way. One of the key moments of Merton's embrace of all people took place on a street corner in Louisville, Kentucky, where he saw a cross-section of humanity waiting for a traffic light to change.

> In Louisville, at the corner of Fourth and Walnut, in the center of the shopping district, I was suddenly overwhelmed with the realization that I loved all those people, that they were mine and I theirs, that we could not be alien to one another even though we were total strangers. It was like waking from a dream of separateness, of

83

spurious self-isolation in a special world, the world of renunciation and supposed holiness. The whole illusion of
a separate holy existence is a dream. (*Conjectures of a
Guilty Bystander*, p. 156)

From his growing contemplative awareness, Merton
learned that he had been led to find God in the world that he
once rejected. He realized what was at stake: "I must look for
my identity, somehow, not only in God but in other men. I will
never be able to find myself if I isolate myself from the rest of
mankind as if I were a different kind of being" (*New Seeds of
Contemplation*, p. 51).

By 1964, he was suggesting that the contemplative life
must not close monks to the outside world but should make
each monk even more sensitive to the needs of the time.
Monks should learn to empathize with the suffering of other
people. Just as all Christians need to serve humankind, so
monks must also. They serve by praying, by providing islands
of retreat, and by witnessing silently that life is more than
power and possessions. In Merton's case, he served his sisters
and brothers by writing books and articles that challenged injustice and violence and by mentoring the many people who
asked his guidance.

Pause: Reflect on times when you might have wanted to
or actually did hide yourself from the travails and needs of
other people.

Merton's Words

When I speak of the contemplative life I do not mean the
institutional cloistered life, the organized life of prayer.
. . . I am talking about a special dimension of inner discipline and experience, a certain integrity and fullness of
personal development, which are not compatible with a
purely external, alienated, busy-busy existence. This does
not mean that they are incompatible with action, with creative work, with dedicated love. On the contrary, these all
go together. A certain depth of disciplined experience is
a necessary ground for fruitful action. Without a more

profound human understanding derived from explo-
ration of the inner ground of human existence, love will
tend to be superficial and deceptive. Traditionally, the
ideas of prayer, meditation and contemplation have been
associated with this deepening of one's personal life and
this expansion of the capacity to understand and serve
others. (*Contemplation in a World of Action*, p. 172)

Reflection

Farmers and financiers, gym instructors and gynecologists,
safety engineers and senators, miners and monks, all who consider themselves Christian are called to serve God's people.
However, in order to truly serve others, writes Merton, we
need to be willing to forgo the results of our service and learn
to live without looking for immediate rewards: "We must be
content to live without watching ourselves live, to work without expecting an immediate reward, to love without an in-
stantaneous satisfaction, and to exist without any special
recognition" (*No Man Is an Island*, p. 121).

This selfless love is one of the fruits of an active prayer
life. The God within us should be the source of our activity,
and we can encounter God through prayer, meditation, and
contemplation. Merton suggests that our ability to love and
serve others depends on our willingness to think less of our
own self-estimation and the estimation of others and, instead,
to rely on the deep spring of God-life within ourself.

In the silence, our inner life meets God's love, the love
that we share in our service. Without prayer, all we may be offering others is an empty heart or a heart filled with conflict.
Merton remarked: "A man who is not at peace with himself
necessarily projects his interior fighting into the society of
those he lives with, and spreads a contagion of conflict all
around him" (*No Man Is an Island*, pp. 120–121).

Prayer and service move in tandem. Service not informed,
guided, and supported by a rich life of prayer is easily weak-
ened, discouraged, and dissipated. Action without contemplation is mere activism. Prayer that does not foster service
and stimulate it is often hollow, self-centered, and effete.

✧ Do you ever nourish the illusion that your wholeness and salvation can be achieved alone and without service to your neighbor? Meditate on this line from Merton: "The whole illusion of a separate holy existence is a dream." Examine your consciousness for times when you have sought or desired a "separate holy existence." Ask God for the grace, like Merton, to love "all those people."

✧ Assess your life of service to your sisters and brothers. In your journal, make four columns with these headings: Family, Friends, Workplace, and Extended Community. Then down the left side of the page, write these acts of charity: Giving Water to the Thirsty, Feeding the Hungry, Welcoming Strangers, Clothing the Naked, Visiting Sick People or Prisoners. Understand each act of charity both literally and metaphorically. For instance, perhaps you have not literally given drink to thirsty people, but maybe you have taught children religion—slaking their thirst for understanding. In each column next to each act of charity, write a brief summary of how you have served God's people.

✧ Recall a time in your life when you were estranged from your inner life and unknowingly caused chaos and anxiety in the lives of others. Let yourself inwardly feel the crisis that occurred. Do not judge yourself; simply allow yourself to remember this time in your life story. Did a new self arise out of the ashes? Have you nourished this inner life? Talk with Jesus about how to be more in touch with his will and his voice speaking within you.

✧ Imagine yourself in a place that represents quiet, solitude, and peacefulness for you. . . . You find a spot in this place where you can sit quietly and let God's presence fill your being. . . . Each time your mind wanders, return to this place where you are encountering God's love. . . . Remain in this place as long as you choose. Let it become a symbol of peace and security. . . . When you find yourself anxious or in the middle of chaos, gently imagine this place where your heart was at peace.

✧ Write a list of times recently when you felt inner peace; entitle it "Sacred Moments." Next, write a list of times when you felt anxious or rushed; entitle it "Chaos." What do these lists reveal about your life? Enter your thoughts in your journal

✧ If you know of some act of service that needs doing but that you have been delaying, do it soon.

God's Word

In the course of their journey he came to a village, and a woman named Martha welcomed him into her house. She had a sister called Mary, who sat down at the Lord's feet and listened to him speaking. Now Martha, who was distracted with all the serving, came to him and said, "Lord, do you not care that my sister is leaving me to do the serving all by myself? Please tell her to help me." But the Lord answered: "Martha, Martha," he said, "you worry and fret about so many things, and yet few are needed, indeed only one. It is Mary who has chosen the better part; and it is not to be taken from her." (Luke 10:38–42)

Closing prayer: O God, give me the courage to find rest in you, especially during the hectic times in my life. Let me learn to keep alive the flame of inner peace and to dwell in your presence so that I can be of service to others. Then, may I be your heart, hands, and voice.

✧ **Meditation 11** ✧

Social Concern

Theme: An illuminating and transforming experience of God can sensitize a person to matters of justice and peace and to the need to speak out and act in radical ways.

Opening prayer: God of peace, let me bring justice and peace to the world and cooperate in shaping human history according to your truth.

About Merton

While at Columbia University, Thomas Merton became involved in student peace movements and volunteered at the Friendship House in Harlem. Before entering the monastery, he chose to apply for the draft status of conscientious objector. Even as a newly converted Catholic, he took the church's social teaching seriously.

His first sixteen years of monastic life removed Merton from many of the troubles of the world and much of the chaos of active life. A slow awakening process began in the late 1950s and grew stronger in the next decade. He immersed himself in the literature of the sixties' culture and reflected on the nuclear devastation of Nagasaki and Hiroshima. He satirized the decision to drop the bomb in an anti-poem entitled "Original Child Bomb."

Appalled by the superpowers squaring off in the Cold War, Merton publicly began criticizing U.S. Catholics for their passivity and the church's silence in regard to the growing nuclear threat. He soon found himself in alliance with Jesuit priest Daniel Berrigan and others of the peace movement. Merton complained about monks who saw no connection between his antiwar stance and his monastic vocation. In a letter to Daniel Berrigan he wrote:

> And now about the monastic life and ideal, in relation to the world. . . . In the name of lifeless and graven letters on parchment, we are told that our life consists in the peaceful and pious meditation on Scripture and a quiet withdrawal from the world. But if one reads the prophets with his ears and eyes open he cannot help recognizing his obligation to shout very loud about God's will, God's truth, and justice of man to man. . . . I don't say it is the dish of every individual monk, but certainly it is incumbent on some monks. (Shannon, ed., *Hidden Ground of Love*, p. 78)

The Catholic pacifists who visited his hermitage encouraged Merton. Working with Gandhi's writings, he developed his own positions on nonviolence. While Merton did not condemn every war, he insisted that nonviolent opposition is the only effective resistance. He expands his definition of nonviolence in a letter to James Forest, a leader in the Catholic peace movement:

> . . . Hence the importance of non-violent people who are really conscientious objectors not only to nuclear war but to *everything* that leads to it or goes with it in the same general atmosphere of violence and criminality. I think the perspectives of the non-violent have to be enlarged in all directions, so that it becomes a genuine and profound spiritual movement, and a force for *life* in a really rotting and corrupt world. How badly this is needed. (Shannon, ed., *Hidden Ground of Love*, p. 273)

The mounting racial tensions in the United States turned Merton's attention to the life of Malcolm X and the speeches of Martin Luther King, Jr. Referring to King, he writes:

Fortunately the Negroes have a leader who is a man of grace, who understands the law of love, who understands the mystery of the greatest secret grace that has been *given to the Negro and to no other.* The grace which the people who first created the spirituals well knew about: the grace of election that made them God's chosen, the grace that elevated them above the meaningless and trivial things of life, even in the midst of terrible and unjust suffering. (*Conjectures of a Guilty Bystander*, p. 112)

Merton traced the problem of ghetto violence not to a few leaders or to rioters but to the illusions embedded in the social structure. He suggested that the only way to stop the turmoil in the streets of the United States was for each individual to cultivate "peace of heart."

Pause: Consider your own sensitivity to injustice. Have you ever felt called to take a stand on a social issue?

Merton's Words

Christian social action is first of all action that discovers religion in politics, religion in work, religion in social programs for better wages, Social Security, etc., not at all to "win the worker for the Church," but because God became man, because every man is potentially Christ, because Christ is our brother, and because we have no right to let our brother live in want, or in degradation, or in any form of squalor whether physical or spiritual. In a word, if we really understood the meaning of Christianity in social life we would see it as part of the redemptive work of Christ, liberating man from misery, squalor, subhuman living conditions, economic or political slavery, ignorance, alienation. (*Conjectures of a Guilty Bystander*, pp. 81–82)

At the root of all war is fear: not so much the fear men have of one another as the fear they have of *everything*. It is not merely that they do not trust one another; they do not even trust themselves. If they are not sure when someone else may turn around and kill them, they are still less sure when they may turn around and kill themselves. They cannot trust anything, because they have ceased to believe in God.

It is not only our hatred of others that is dangerous but also and above all our hatred of ourselves: particularly that hatred of ourselves which is too deep and too powerful to be consciously faced. For it is this which makes us see our own evil in others and unable to see it in ourselves. (*New Seeds of Contemplation*, p. 112)

Reflection

To grow in love and to have the strength and wisdom to challenge the fear within ourself, as well as social ills, requires prayer, meditation, and contemplation. These keep us focused on God's will, God's love, God's invitation to full life. Prayer, meditation, and contemplation give us knowledge of a "hidden ground of love," says Merton, where all humanity is united in God. Experiencing such love urges us to confront and transform racism, violence, fear, and oppression.

In effect, Merton recognized that without spiritual transformation we will continue to turn against one another. Ignoring our common ground as human beings, we compete, suspect, and end in conflict with one another. Only love will overcome the social problems of contemporary society, because only love transcends individual interests. Merton hails the divine life that exists in everyone, calling us to discover the unity that binds us all together.

Without a life of prayer, the hollow values of popular culture and dysfunctional traditions can infect our souls and weaken our wills. The person God created us to be, the person grounded in love, can be sacrificed for a self that eagerly defends destructive myths like racial superiority or corrupt values like "looking out for number one."

Action for justice and peacemaking are integral to full Christian life. No one who loves Christ—whether monk or model, senator or salesperson—can be exempt from putting love into action for the good of humankind. As Merton says, "Christianity in social life . . . [is] part of the redemptive work of Christ."

✧ Meditate on the second reading in "Merton's Words." Examine your consciousness using these questions:

+ What do I fear? (You may even want to write a list.) Is Merton right when he says that I fear myself?

+ When has my fear caused me to be defensive, mean, arrogant, envious, even violent?

+ Are there times when I hate myself? When? With whom? Why?

+ What do I hate in others? Is this something I fear in myself?

Open your heart to Christ now. Ask for his guidance on how to be liberated from your fear and hatred. Pray for the grace you need.

✧ Be aware that we perpetuate injustice by aimless consumption, whether physical or mental. Take an inventory of the magazines, books, films, videos, appliances, wardrobes, and recreational equipment that you use and consider whether they hinder your awareness of other people and of yourself. Do your possessions make you fearful of other people? Would simplifying your life free you from some of your fear?

✧ What are the sources of anger in your life at present?

+ Are you suppressing your anger and allowing it to control your emotional and spiritual life?

+ Make peace, if only through an imaginative dialog, with the source of your anger.

+ Strategize about dealing with your anger. As with stress, three ways are open for us to deal with anger. We can change the situation; we can get out of the situation; or we can change our attitude about the situation. After examining your anger, which of these three options would be optimal? After praying for God's grace, act to cope with your anger.

+ Ask God in prayer to heal your inner wounds of anger.

✧ List the voices that you hear crying out for justice, peace, liberation, or relief in our time. Choose one of the voices that speaks most powerfully to you and speak to it. Create a dialog that allows the voice to speak to you in a personal way. If the voice comes from a group of people like the poor or the homeless, focus your attention on an individual (real or imaginary) that represents the group. Continue the dialog until it ends naturally. Then ask yourself the following questions:

✦ How did the dialog heighten my awareness of the person(s) in need?

✦ What did I feel when the dialog ended?

✦ Did the dialog motivate me toward any action? If so, describe it.

✦ What am I doing and what more should I do to create a more just and peaceful world?

✧ Our addiction to war and violence can only be overcome through "peace of heart." Pray Merton's "Prayer for Peace" in the "Closing prayer," pausing for silence or to add your own reflections when you feel the prayer invites a response from you.

God's Word

In the evening of that same day, the first day of the week, the doors were closed in the room where the disciples were, for fear of the Jews. Jesus came and stood among them. He said to them, "Peace be with you," and after saying this, he showed them his hands and his side. The disciples were filled with joy at seeing the Lord, and he said to them again, "Peace be with you." (John 20:19–21)

Closing prayer:

Grant us prudence in proportion to our power,
Wisdom in proportion to our science,
Humaneness in proportion to our wealth and might,
And bless our earnest will to help all races and peoples
     to travel, in friendship with us,
Along the road to justice, liberty, and lasting peace:
But grant us above all to see that our ways
     are not necessarily your ways,
That we cannot fully penetrate the mystery
     of your designs

And that the very storm of power now raging
    on this earth
Reveals your hidden will and your inscrutable decision.
Grant us to see your face in the lightning
    of this cosmic storm,
O God of holiness, merciful to men:
Grant us to seek peace where it is truly found!
    In your will, O God, is our peace!
        AMEN

(Thomas Merton, "Prayer for Peace,"
in *A Thomas Merton Reader*, ed. McDonnell, p. 284)

✧ **Meditation 12** ✧

The Person of Christ

Theme: The person of Jesus Christ is central to any Christian community. Relationship with Christ is the source of a joyous, full life.

Opening prayer: May I be open to Christ in the Gospel and in his daily revelations in my life. Come, Jesus, friend, wisdom, shepherd, light, and life!

About Merton

While Thomas Merton was at Columbia University, his Hindu monk friend, Bramachari, counseled him to read Saint Augustine's *Confessions*, and *The Imitation of Christ*, by Thomas à Kempis. This piece of advice eventually led him to add a copy of *The Imitation of Christ* to his collection and to explore the mystery of Christ in the context of scholastic theology, especially with the help of his professor friend Daniel Walsh.

Merton's previous experience of the image of Christ came when, at age eighteen, he vacationed in Rome. The Byzantine mosaics of Christ caught his attention. "And now for the first time in my life I began to find out something of Who this Person was that men called Christ. . . . It was in Rome that my conception of Christ was formed" (*Seven Storey Mountain*, p. 109).

Later, when he was thinking about converting to Catholicism, Merton heard a sermon at the Church of Corpus Christi in New York City, which put him in touch again with the mystery of the Incarnation. He recalled the ancient Roman mosaics of Christ that had so moved him. When Merton left Corpus Christi filled with wonder at the God-Man present on the altar, he felt transformed by this moment of grace. "All I know is that I walked in a new world. Even the ugly buildings of Columbia were transfigured in it, and everywhere was peace in these streets designed for violence and noise" (*Seven Storey Mountain*, p. 211).

In the monastery, the liturgical and communal life, the emphasis on the Scriptures, and the monastic spiritual tradition heightened his experience of Christ. He wrote: "The whole meaning of the monastic life flows from the mystery of the incarnation. We come to the monastery, drawn by the action of the Holy Spirit, seeking eternal life. Eternal life is the life of God, given to us in Christ" (*Monastic Journey*, p. 33).

Through the Incarnation, Christ brought about the transformation of humanity. Merton recognized that Christ's image is in each of us, and the task of the Christian is to uncover the image in the self as well as in other people.

> From the moment that we have responded by faith and charity to His love for us, a supernatural union of our souls with His indwelling Divine Person gives us a participation in His divine sonship and nature. A "new being" is brought into existence. I become a "new man" and this new man, spiritually and mystically one identity, is at once Christ and myself. (*New Seeds of Contemplation*, p. 158)

Merton's vision of all life as sacramental flowed from his love of Christ made flesh. His belief in serving others and involvement in social reform evolved from his commitment to the presence of Christ in the world. Even his attraction to Asian religions and his journey to the East influenced his awareness of the presence of Christ. Describing his meeting with lamas, Sufis, and Buddhist monks at the end of a circular letter to his friends, he wrote: "In my contacts with these new friends I also feel consolation in my own faith in Christ and His indwelling presence. I hope and believe He may be present in the hearts of all of us" (Burton, Hart, and Laughlin, eds., *Asian Journal*, p. 325).

Pause: Ponder how you have developed your relationship with Christ.

Merton's Words

Here it is essential to remember that for a Christian "the word of the Cross" is nothing theoretical, but a stark and existential experience of union with Christ in His death in order to share in His resurrection. To fully "hear" and "receive" the word of the Cross means much more than simple assent to the dogmatic proposition that Christ died for our sins. It means to be "nailed to the Cross with Christ," so that the ego-self is no longer the principle of our deepest actions, which now proceed from Christ living in us. "I live, now not I, but Christ lives in me." (Gal. 2:19–20; see also Romans 8:5–17) To receive the word of the Cross means the acceptance of a complete self-emptying, a *Kenosis*, in union with the self-emptying of Christ "obedient unto death." (Phil. 2:5–11) It is essential to true Christianity that this experience of the Cross and of self-emptying be central in the life of the Christian so that he may fully receive the Holy Spirit and know (again by experience) all the riches of God in and through Christ. (*Zen and the Birds of Appetite*, pp. 55–56)

Reflection

The purpose of all prayer is to bring about a loving union with Christ, the incarnate Word. At one point Merton warned, "No one can dismiss the Man Christ from his interior life on the pretext that he has now entered by higher contemplation into direct communication with the Word" (*New Seeds of Contemplation*, p. 152). The Risen Christ cannot be reduced to concepts and images; they are always too small to contain the person of Christ.

Whether gazing at images or attending in silent contemplation, Christ should be the center of prayer. Merton remarked, "We read the Gospels not merely to get a picture or an idea of Christ but to enter in and pass through the words of revelation to establish, by faith, a vital contact with the Christ Who dwells in our souls as God" (*New Seeds of Contemplation,* p. 156). All forms of prayer—liturgical prayer, meditation, vocal prayer, or contemplation—nurture our relationship with the source of all truth and life, Jesus Christ.

Merton directs us to Christ at the center of the heart. We find our worth by discovering through prayer that we are loved by Christ. In response to this love, we grow in the inward presence of Christ and learn to love others more fully.

✧ Read "Merton's Words" again. Then reflect on the image of Christ as the ray of God's light. You may want to meditate on this image while watching a sunrise or sunset. Pray these words to begin and end your meditation and if you become distracted: "Jesus Christ, Light of the World."

✧ When have you experienced the personal presence of Christ, the friendship of Christ in your heart? Recall the event and let it lead you into resting in Christ's presence for as long as you can.

✧ Practice repeating the name of Jesus throughout the day, allowing it to deepen your appreciation of Christ's personal love for you and his unique call to you.

✧ How is Christ calling you to imitate him in your life? For example, think of the Spirit of Christ as the Spirit of Love and ask yourself how you can better express this love in a way that is unique to you.

✧ Picture the love of Christ as breath that flows through you. Now concentrate on your breathing and think of the mystery of Christ's love renewing itself in you each moment of your existence.

✧ Reflect on this comment from Merton: "Christ develops your life into Himself like a photograph" (*New Seeds of Contemplation*, p. 162). Write a prayer when you are finished.

God's Word

Even before creation was the Word.
The Word dwelled with God.
Indeed, the Word is God.
All of life came from the Word,
And the Word is light to all creatures,
an inextinguishable, eternal light for the world.
                                        (Adapted from John 1:1–5)

Closing prayer: Spirit of Christ, I may be unaware of your constant presence dwelling within me, but let me recognize you at least in the people and events you send to me day after day. Let me acknowledge your presence when your name is spoken in the everyday routine, and let my heart burn for you.

Community Life

Theme: Spiritual growth is inseparable from a nurturing, challenging, and celebrative community life.

Opening prayer: O God, let my prayer flower from my relationships with other people. Let me be more sensitive to your revelation in the truth and love of my communities.

About Merton

Thomas Merton's personality was too independent and creative not to rock the boat of community life at times. He found it difficult to fit in because he was sensitive to any inauthenticity found in the monastic community. His wit and talent for satire gave an edge to his social criticism both in the monastery and later when he wrote about issues of peace and justice.

Nevertheless, the testimony of his own Trappist brothers make clear that he was well loved in the community and had a special affection for members who went unnoticed. One young monk, John Eudes Bamberger, looked to him as a spiritual mentor and found that rather than Merton being reserved and pious, "he was a very outgoing person with an obvious ease with relationships, very approachable, with a great sense of humor" (Paul Wilkes, ed., *Merton by Those Who Knew Him Best*, p. 116).

Merton found joy at the heart of community life. He described the monastery in this way: "[It] is a school—a school in which we learn from God how to be happy. Our happiness consists in sharing the happiness of God, the perfection of His unlimited freedom, the perfection of His love" (*Seven Storey Mountain*, p. 372).

Merton's community extended beyond the monastery's walls. He maintained many friendships through voluminous correspondence and the visits of friends to the monastery. Merton was a wise, caring, and playful friend.

James Forest, a peace activist and former editor of *The Catholic Worker* newspaper, told the story of one of his visits to Merton. When Forest and a friend arrived at Gethsemani, Forest went to the chapel to pray. His companion collapsed from exhaustion in the guest house. As Forest tried to pray in the chapel, he heard great bursts of laughter. Finding concentration impossible, he followed the laughter back to his friend's room. When he opened the door, he found his friend laughing heartily, but "so was this monk [Merton] on the floor who was in his black and white robes, big leather belt around him, feet up in the air, clutching his belly, his face as red as a tomato" (Wilkes, ed., *Those Who Knew Him Best*, p. 49).

Merton could be a playful joker, but he took monastic community and its future seriously. In October 1968, he told participants at the Calcutta Conference: "This monastic 'work' or 'discipline' is not merely an individual affair. It is at once personal and communal" (Burton, Hart, and Laughlin, eds., *Asian Journal*, p. 310).

Until the end of his life, Merton worked on redefining the monastic community for the twentieth century. He believed in a truthful communion with other people, both monks and friends. He also believed that deep within all human beings existed a heart open to union in God's truth and love.

On the day that the news of Merton's death reached Gethsemani, an elderly monk for whom Merton had special affection found a postcard from Merton waiting for him in the refectory. When Merton was buried at the monastery cemetery among his brothers, he rested among friends.

Pause: What impact would separation from the people you love have on your spiritual journey?

Merton's Words

We do not exist for ourselves alone, and it is only when we are fully convinced of this fact that we begin to love ourselves properly and thus also love others. What do I mean by loving ourselves properly? I mean, first of all, desiring to live, accepting life as a very great gift and a great good, not because of what it gives us, but because of what it enables us to give to others. . . .

Every Christian is part of my own body, because we are members of Christ. What I do is also done for them and with them and by them. What they do is done in me and by me and for me. But each one of us remains responsible for his own share in the life of the whole body. Charity cannot be what it is supposed to be as long as I do not see that my life represents my own allotment in the life of a whole supernatural organism to which I belong. (*No Man Is an Island*, pp. xx, xxii)

Reflection

Thomas Merton emphasized that the inner life is not isolated but is most fully lived in a reciprocal relationship with a community. Spiritual stability requires sharing in communal life. Even Merton's well-known preference for a hermit's existence never uprooted him from the ground of monastic life.

For Merton, the discovery of God as the authentic center of life coincides with the awakening to our capacity to love other people. This is a paradox of the spiritual life: "A man cannot enter into the deepest center of himself and pass through that center into God, unless he is able to pass entirely out of himself and empty himself and give himself to other people in the purity of selfless love" (*New Seeds of Contemplation*, p. 64).

To think that our spiritual life can be separated from the people around us is an illusion. We are one body in Christ. We can truly understand and care for other people only by loving the God who completely understands and unconditionally loves them.

Authentic love readily expresses itself in concrete service to other people. Merton reached out to his brothers in the monastery through his care and teaching. He reached out in love to the human family through his letters, books, poems, and art. He challenges us to make peace, bring justice, and love our sisters and brothers in specific, tangible ways. He also reminds us that charity withers unless it is rooted and watered by our relationship with the God who is love.

✧ Read "Merton's Words" again and recall the ways in which you have expressed to other people the giftedness of your life.

Thank God for the giftedness of your life. Let your gratitude be complete.

Express your sorrow for the times when you refused to share your giftedness with other people. Let your contrition be complete.

Finally, praise God for the goodness of your being, for all the gifts that you have been given to share with others.

✧ Think of an unnoticed or forgotten person in your family or community who would benefit from your attention. Find a way that you can serve or enrich this person's life without imposing yourself on him or her.

✧ In his translation of one of the greatest of the Taoist philosophers, Chuang Tzu, Merton explored the topic of relationships with others in community. Read the following stanza and consider which of your relationships are "friendships with wise men [and women]" and which are "friendships of fools":

The friendship of wise men
Is tasteless as water.
The friendship of fools
Is sweet as wine.
But the tastelessness of the wise
Brings true affection
And the savor of fools' company
Ends in hatred.

(*The Way of Chuang Tzu*, p. 117)

Thank God for the wise friends in your life. Pray for the foolish ones.

✧ Typically we belong to many communities: a family, a civic community, a parish, a community of friends, a small prayer group, and so on. Choose an image or symbol that represents community experience for you. Draw the image. Take time to be present to it, and allow it to be present to you.

✦ Recall your earliest memory of being part of a community. What feelings do you remember?

✦ What important community experiences have you had since childhood?

✦ What have you received from your participation in your present community or communities?

✦ What gifts have you added to the community experience?

✦ What kind of community life do you envision for yourself in the future?

✧ Merton wrote that "the lives of all the men we meet and know are woven into our own destiny, together with the lives of many we shall never know on earth" (*No Man Is an Island* [1955], p. 12). On a piece of paper, with a pencil, draw a rough outline of a tapestry or weaving that you feel represents your life in process. Then write the name of each person who has influenced your life, past or present, on each thread of the tapestry. When you have finished writing, recall each person on the tapestry. Linger over memory of them. Relax. Breathe slowly and deeply. Close your eyes and see the tapestry again. Celebrate the people who have woven themselves into the fabric of your life and destiny.

✧ Merton loved to laugh and enjoy the company of other people. Have you done so recently?

✦ Plan a dinner with friends you have not seen for a while. Use the opportunity to show your appreciation for their friendship.

✦ Call a friend you have neglected to talk to for some time.

✦ Write a letter to a friend you know is experiencing a setback in his or her life.

✦ Spend time with someone with whom you can be playful.

✦ Reflect on the many ways you can use your gifts to build community among the many people in your life.

God's Word

Those who love me will keep my word. God will love them and dwell among them. . . . So live in my love by keeping my commandments. (Adapted from John 14:23, 15:9–10)

Remain in me, as I in you.
As a branch cannot bear fruit all by itself,
unless it remains part of the vine,
neither can you unless you remain in me.

(John 15:4)

Closing prayer: O God, deepen my awareness of my relationship with the human community. Give me the courage and compassion not to escape the problems and suffering of the human family but to affirm the value of human life and the transcendent dimension of each person I encounter.

The Prophetic Call

Theme: We who participate in the world must also share in the responsibility for its growth. Sometimes we are called to be God's prophetic voice.

Opening prayer: O God, heighten my awareness of my responsibility to humanity and let me have a genuine concern for the world in which I live. If I am called to be a prophet, give me strength and send me forth.

About Merton

The prophet has a message that others need to hear. In unique ways, each Christian has been called to be a prophet. For instance, the monk, to be a true contemplative, must witness to Christ in the world. In the *Sign of Jonas*, Thomas Merton suggested that the monastic vocation was truly a prophetic one:

> A monk can always legitimately and significantly compare himself to a prophet, because the monks are the heirs of the prophets. The prophet is a man whose whole life is a living witness of the providential action of God in the world. Every prophet is a sign and a witness of Christ. Every monk, in whom Christ lives, and in whom all the prophecies are therefore fulfilled, is a witness and a sign

of the Kingdom of God. Even our mistakes are eloquent, more than we know. ([1956], p. 20)

Merton believed that his life as a monk was an eschatological sign pointing to a better future and calling others to make their own hope a reality. In the same manner as biblical prophets, Merton announced a new day of the Redeemer for a contemporary society that was experiencing the downfall of its structures and ideals. On 22 November 1963, when President John F. Kennedy was shot in Dallas, Merton condemned the act as "one more in a whole long series of senseless, brutal, stupid, pathological killings" (*Conjectures of a Guilty Bystander*, pp. 343–344).

During a time of political, social, and religious upheaval that began with World War II and included Vatican Council II, Merton's prophetic voice cried out:

It is my intention to make my entire life a rejection of, a protest against the crimes and injustices of war and political tyranny which threaten to destroy the whole race of man and the world with him. By my monastic life and vows I am saying NO to all the concentration camps, the aerial bombardments, the staged political trials, the judicial murders, the racial injustices, the economic tyrannies, and the whole socio-economic apparatus which seems geared for nothing but global destruction in spite of all its fair words in favor of peace. I make monastic silence a protest against the lies of politicians, propagandists and agitators, and when I speak it is to deny that my faith and my Church can ever seriously be aligned with these forces of injustice and destruction. (*Honorable Reader*, pp. 65–66)

Not long before he died, Merton addressed a gathering of Christian monks and nuns concerning monastic renewal. He challenged his audience by recalling the words of a Tibetan lama who had to flee his country because of Chinese persecution: "From now on, Brother, everybody stands on his own feet" (Burton, Hart, and Laughlin, eds., *Asian Journal*, p. 338). Merton told his audience that monks and nuns must take responsibility for the prophetic message of Jesus, not rely on external structures for support. They must face the road ahead by becoming prophets.

Pause: Ponder this question: How is God urging you to be a prophet, one who calls for repentance and announces the Reign of God?

Merton's Words

The great historical event, the coming of the Kingdom, is made clear and is "realized" in proportion as Christians themselves live the life of the Kingdom in the circumstances of their own place and time. The saving grace of God in the Lord Jesus is proclaimed to man existentially in the love, the openness, the simplicity, the humility and the self-sacrifice of Christians. By their example of a truly Christian understanding of the world, expressed in a living and active application of the Christian faith to the human problems of their own time, Christians manifest the love of Christ for men (Jn 13:35, 17:21), and by that fact make him visibly present in the world. (*Faith and Violence*, p. 16)

Reflection

In a poem entitled "The Tower of Babel: A Morality," Merton criticizes the city that people build to create a diversion from the boredom of their unsatisfactory existence (*Collected Poems*, p. 247). The tower of Babel and the city collapse. Then the Prophet reminds them of a real city, a "City of God," which will rise from the ashes of the old one when people accept that truth can only be found in God. All Christians should turn away from the false city that will eventually collapse. We are called to be citizens of an eternal city—the City of God that transcends political boundaries—and to become witnesses of a new reality, a rebirth of human beings and society.

According to Merton, "The prophet is a [person] whose whole life is a living witness of the providential action of God in the world." The monk can be the prophet who teaches that, in fact, life is more than possessions, status, striving, and pleasure-seeking. Only God is enough. Other Christians can give prophetic voice to the Good News in their own way.

Merton traces the prophetic vocation to the desert where the Israelites wandered for forty years, learning how to love God. The desert taught Israel to remain true to the all-merciful God when Israel was tempted to stray:

> Recovery of the spirit of the desert meant a return to fidelity, to charity, to fraternal union; it meant the destruction of the inequalities and oppressions dividing rich and poor; conversion to justice and equity meant the return to the true sabbath. (*Disputed Questions*, p. 224)

Faith in God draws each of us into the desert of our hearts, where we learn to believe that Christ's hidden power works within us. In the desert, we learn that only Christ can give the healing water that completely slakes our thirst. Discovery of this truth compels us to proclaim the Good News to others. The desert vocation demands a great deal, urging us to turn the world upside down. Each of us, once we take this faith journey seriously, becomes a prophet.

✧ Slowly reread "Merton's Words," pondering each sentence, its meaning, and its challenge to you. Talk with Jesus about the passage. What is Jesus calling you to do?

✧ If you could choose one woman or man who models the prophetic role to you, who would it be?
✦ Describe the characteristics you admire in this person.
✦ Which of these characteristics could you incorporate into your own life?
✦ Take some time in silence to reflect on the ways you can answer the call to be a prophet.

✧ Merton critiqued the anti-spiritual, herd mentality that pervades our culture. List the aspects of our social structure, its norms and customs, its values and expectations, that you find a hindrance to your own spiritual journey. Choose two aspects and reflect on the ways they have stunted your spiritual growth. Now list ways in which you can share the responsibility to help our social structure become more centered in Christ. Pray for the courage you need to be prophetic in these ways.

✧ Recall a person who suffers from a form of injustice. Bring to mind his or her face and situation. Speak the person's name, repeating it with each breath. Allow yourself to gradually become one with this person, entering her or his suffering. Ask God what you can do to help the person and for the will to do what you can. Pray for the person. Finally, rest in the silence of your faith.

✧ As Christians, we are called to oppose injustice according to the demands of our conscience. Ponder news reports for the last couple of days that clearly narrate instances of injustice. List some practical ways you can combat injustice in your daily life: at and through your work, at home, in the larger community. Act on one or two of these.

✧ Merton suggested that we cannot develop an inner life without concern for the suffering of others and without becoming responsible for others in need. Repeat the following phrase as many times as necessary, answering it differently with each repetition: "I, (your name), promise to reach out to _____." Now say a short prayer asking forgiveness for all the times you failed to take responsibility for helping others.

God's Word

> A voice cries, "Prepare in the desert
> a way for Yahweh.
> Make a straight highway for our God
> across the wastelands.
> Let every valley be filled in,
> every mountain and hill be levelled,
> every cliff become a plateau,
> every escarpment a plain;
> then the glory of Yahweh will be revealed
> and all humanity will see it together,
> for the mouth of Yahweh has spoken."

(Isaiah 40:3–5)

Closing prayer: God of justice and mercy, let me hear your word spoken in my heart and give me the strength to speak it to others in your name.

✧ **Meditation 15** ✧

The Quest for Unity

Theme: Merton believed that Christians are called to unity with all of humankind. Therefore, they should seek to discover truths found in various religions, while being faithful to and growing in their own religious tradition.

Opening prayer: O God of truth, O hidden ground of love, let me not only learn more about my own religion but lead me, a pilgrim, toward a better understanding of other ancient spiritual traditions. With a deeper understanding of our similarities, may I be further united with all my sisters and brothers.

About Merton

As Thomas Merton's contemplative life intensified, he became more aware that all other religions shared his goal: union with "Being, call it Atman, call it Pneuma . . . or Silence. . . . The happiness of being at one with everything in that hidden ground of Love for which there can be no explanations" (Shannon, ed., *Hidden Ground of Love*, p. 115).

Benefiting from Vatican Council II's openness to other traditions, Merton eagerly explored Eastern mysticism, especially Zen. He defended Eastern mysticism against claims that it denied life, led only to self-preoccupation, and attempted to escape reality. He realized that Eastern meditation practices stripped away illusions of the false self and created an authentic link to the "hidden ground of Love."

In Merton's mind, Eastern religions could help Westerners become aware of the depths of their own tradition and might save Western religions from stagnation. Eastern religious tradition could help temper the passion of the West for money, power, militarism, and self-gratification by offering reverence for silence, meditation, peace, and compassion.

In 1968, Merton journeyed to the Orient as a pilgrim, returning to a place that he had already explored through his reading and meditation. The pilgrim who had meditated on Eastern mystical classics and corresponded with scholars and practitioners of Eastern religions was going "home" for spiritual nourishment (Shannon, *Silent Lamp*, p. 9). In his *Asian Journal*, Merton wrote: "I come as a pilgrim who is anxious to obtain not just information, not just 'facts' about other monastic traditions, but to drink from ancient sources of monastic vision and experience" (Burton, Hart, and Laughlin, eds., pp. 312–313).

Merton particularly found the Zen attitude toward life paralleled in the poverty, solitude, and emptiness of the Christian Desert Fathers and Mothers. In meeting Dr. Daisetsu T. Suzuki, who popularized Zen meditation in the West, Merton found "someone who, in a tradition completely different from my own, had matured, had become complete and found his way" (*Zen and the Birds of Appetite*, p. 62).

Zen meditation's ability to cut through the illusions created by the ego and to affirm life was especially attractive to Merton. He found no contradiction between Zen and Christianity at the level of pure experience. Merton wrote:

> Thus with all due deference to the vast doctrinal differences between Buddhism and Christianity, and preserving intact all respect for the claims of the different religions: in no way mixing up the Christian "vision of God" with Buddhist "enlightenment," we can nevertheless say that the two have this psychic "limitlessness" in common. And they tend to describe it in much the same language. It is now "emptiness," now "dark night," now

"perfect freedom," now "no-mind" now "poverty." (*Zen and the Birds of Appetite*, p. 8)

Merton did not agree that mystics throughout the world experience the same things and transcend cultures and traditions through their religious practices. Nevertheless, in his conversations with great teachers and monks such as the Dalai Lama, he found common elements among the different traditions. He especially found that monks in every culture have a serious desire for inner transformation and eventual union with the Absolute, which is cultivated by ongoing discipline. The authentic religious quest, according to Merton, uncovers one's own radical identity and leads to a sense of unity with other traditions. In other words, if we take our own spiritual journey seriously, we will inevitably find companions from other traditions along the way.

Pause: Ask yourself: Do I respect other people's spiritual journey toward the Hidden Ground of Love?

Merton's Words

We know that the Desert Fathers of Egypt . . . sought a perfect purity of heart, and for this reason they avoided making learning or conceptual knowledge too much of an end in itself. We find in Zen an analogous striving for non-attachment, and an apophatic contemplation which is summed up in the term "no-mind." . . . But the "emptiness" and "objectlessness" of the Zen way of "no-mind" must be well understood, for in such a delicate matter the slightest error is disastrous. To become attached to emptiness itself and to an imaginary "purity of heart" that is conceived as an object which one can attain is to miss the target altogether, even though it may seem to be the highest point of the mystical life. (*Mystics and Zen Masters*, p. 221)

At one point in his Asian journey, Merton went to see the rock sculptures of the Buddha in Polonnaruwa, Sri Lanka. This is his account of the moving experience.

I am able to approach the Buddhas barefoot and undisturbed, my feet in wet grass, wet sand. Then the silence of the extraordinary faces. The great smiles. Huge and yet subtle. Filled with every possibility, questioning nothing, knowing everything, rejecting nothing. . . . For the doctrinaire, the mind that needs well-established positions, such peace, such silence, can be frightening. I was knocked over with a rush of relief and thankfulness at the *obvious* clarity of the figures, the clarity and fluidity of shape and line, the design. . . .

Looking at these figures I was suddenly, almost forcibly, jerked clean out of the habitual, half-tied vision of things, and an inner clearness, clarity, as if exploding from the rocks themselves, became evident and obvious. (Burton, Hart, and Laughlin, eds., *Asian Journal*, pp. 233, 235)

Reflection

By 1967, Merton had turned his attention to monastic renewal. He was convinced that the future monastic should be taught not only Catholic Tradition but non-Christian traditions as well. Beyond a mere intellectual grasp of these religions, the monastic should identify with them and discover their true meaning, praying not only the Christian Bible, but the Upanishads and the Buddhist sutras. Merton's goal was to recognize the contemplative mode of perception that characterizes Eastern and Western traditions.

In the East, Merton found sympathy for the contemplative ideals that the West had bartered away in pursuit of technological dominance, money, and power. He felt strongly that dialog between the East and West would renew the common ground of contemplative experience in all religious.

Particularly during the last ten years of his life, Merton concentrated on a vision of humankind united in understanding and love. He believed that those in the advanced stages of spiritual growth of every tradition, whether Buddhist, Hindu, or Christian, experienced communion in a transcendent reality.

Merton appreciated the wisdom of religious traditions and searched for common ground among them, yet he remained a devout Catholic and Cistercian monk to the end of his life. He encouraged all Christians to reinforce their own belief in the unity of all humanity. Without hiding beyond religious prejudices, Christians should seek a common bond with other men and women who journey toward the truth.

✧ Merton found a common ground between Zen practice and the tradition of Christian spirituality that emphasizes the "dark night" of a soul, during which it learns to love God above all else.

✦ Repeat the phrase, "My God, my God why have you forsaken me?" (Matthew 27:46), and ponder the absolute abandonment that Jesus felt when he uttered these words.

✦ Then concentrate on these words:

> And for this God raised him high,
> and gave him the name
> which is above all other names.
>
> (Philippians 2:9)

Reflect on emptiness as the path to fullness; nothingness as the path to everything.

✧ The way of non-action—the gentle art of doing nothing, of being less occupied with doing things and more with letting things happen—is found throughout Eastern religions.

✦ Reflect on the following passage:

> "In all truth I tell you,
> when you were young
> you put on your own belt
> and walked where you liked;
> but when you grow old
> you will stretch out your hands,
> and somebody else will put a belt round you
> and take you where you would rather not go."
>
> (John 21:18)

✦ In the first part of their life, most people try to take control over their destiny through decisions and actions. List the ways that you took charge of your life in the beginning, the decisions you made, the goals you set.

✦ In the next stage of their life, many people become less preoccupied with control and more open to their inner life. List examples in your life that demonstrate your letting go of control: for instance, sickness due to injury or age, disappointments, setbacks.

✦ Look over the passage from John, and and then read your lists. Write your reflections in your journal.

✧ Reflect on these lines from the Hindu scriptures: "Behold the universe in the glory of God: and all that lives and moves on earth. Leaving the transient, find joy in the Eternal: set not your heart on another's possession" (Juan Mascaró, trans., *The Upanishads*, p. 49).

✦ How does this excerpt remind you of the Christian Scriptures? How is it different?

✦ How does this reading apply to your own spiritual path?

✦ Ask God to give you wisdom to find the Gospel message in other sources like this one from the Hindu tradition.

✧ Zen speaks of the existence of one's original face before one's parents were born; to discover this original face is to find enlightenment. Compare this image with these words addressed to Jeremiah:

> Before I formed you in the womb I knew you;
> before you came to birth I consecrated you;
> I appointed you as prophet to the nations.
>
> (Jeremiah 1:5)

On hearing these words, Jeremiah experienced his true self in God. This is the self that is not bound by space and time, the self, as Merton says, that is not limited by illusion.

✦ Reflect on the obstacles that keep you from recognizing your original face.

✦ If your original face is a mirror (the mirror mind of Buddhism), think of it as reflecting a face other than your own: the face of God.

✦ Meditate on yourself as uniquely loved and chosen by God. Enter the meditation in your journal.

God's Word

He also said, "What can we say that the [reign] is like? What parable can we find for it? It is like a mustard seed which, at the time of its sowing, is the smallest of all the seeds on earth. Yet once it is sown it grows into the biggest shrub of them all and puts out big branches so that the birds of the air can shelter in its shade." (Mark 4:30–32)

This is the Spirit that is in my heart, smaller than a grain of rice, or a grain of barley, or a grain of mustard-seed, or a grain of canary-seed, or the kernel of a grain of canary-seed. This is the Spirit that is in my heart, greater than the earth, greater than the sky, greater than heaven itself, greater than all these worlds. (Mascaró, trans., *The Upanishads*, p. 114)

Closing prayer:

Oh God, in accepting one another wholeheartedly, fully, completely, we accept You, and we thank You, and we adore You, and we love You with our whole being, because our being is in Your being, our spirit is rooted in Your spirit. Fill us then with love, and let us be bound together with love as we go our diverse ways, united in this one spirit which makes You present in the world, and which makes You witness to the ultimate reality that is love. Love has overcome. Love is victorious. Amen. (Thomas Merton's closing prayer at the First Spiritual Summit Conference in Calcutta, India; Burton, Hart, and Laughlin, eds., *Asian Journal*, pp. 318–319)

UNITY

✦ For Further Reading ✦

Selected Books by Thomas Merton

The Collected Poems. New York: New Directions, 1977.

Conjectures of a Guilty Bystander. Garden City, NY: Image Books, 1968.

Contemplation in a World of Action. Garden City, NY: Image Books, 1973.

Contemplative Prayer. Garden City, NY: Image Books, 1971.

Faith and Violence. Notre Dame, IN: University of Notre Dame Press, 1968.

Mystics and Zen Masters. New York: Dell Publishing Company, 1967.

New Seeds of Contemplation. New York: New Directions, 1962.

No Man Is an Island. New York: Harcourt Brace Jovanovich, Publishers, 1978.

The Seven Storey Mountain. New York: Harcourt Brace Jovanovich, Publishers, 1948.

Thoughts in Solitude. Garden City, NY: Image Books, 1968.

The Way of Chuang Tzu. New York: New Directions, 1969.

The Wisdom of the Desert. New York: New Directions, 1970.

Collections of Merton's Writing and Correspondence

Burton, Naomi, Patrick Hart, and James Laughlin, eds. *The Asian Journal of Thomas Merton*. New York: New Directions, 1973.

Daggy, Robert E., ed. *The Road to Joy: Letters of Thomas Merton to New and Old Friends*. New York: Farrar, Straus, Giroux, 1989.

Hart, Patrick, ed. *The School of Charity: Letters of Thomas Merton on Religious Renewal and Spiritual Direction*. New York: Farrar, Straus, Giroux, 1990.

McDonnell, Thomas P., ed. *A Thomas Merton Reader*. Garden City, NY: Image Books, 1974.

Merton, Thomas. *A Vow of Conversation: Journals 1964–1965*. Edited by Naomi Burton Stone. New York: Farrar, Straus, Giroux, 1988.

Shannon, William H., ed. *The Hidden Ground of Love: The Letters of Thomas Merton on Religious Experience and Social Concerns*. New York: Farrar, Straus, Giroux, 1985.

Books about Thomas Merton

Furlong, Monica. *Merton: A Biography*. San Francisco: Harper and Row, Publishers, 1981.

Malits, Elena. *The Solitary Explorer: Thomas Merton's Transforming Journey*. San Francisco: Harper and Row, Publishers, 1980.

Mott, Michael. *The Seven Mountains of Thomas Merton*. Boston: Houghton Mifflin, 1984. (Authorized biography)

Pennington, M. Basil. *Thomas Merton, Brother Monk*. San Francisco: Harper and Row, Publishers, 1987.

Shannon, William H. *Silent Lamp: The Thomas Merton Story*. New York: Crossroad Publishing Company, 1992.

The excerpts on pages 26, 51, 55, 56, and 78 are from *A Vow of Conversation: Journals 1964–1965*, by Thomas Merton, edited by Naomi Burton Stone (New York: Farrar, Straus, Giroux, 1988), pages 206; 112, 108, and 155; 152; 113; 156 and 95; respectively. Copyright © 1988 by the Merton Legacy Trust. Used by permission of the publisher.

The excerpts on pages 28–29, 29, 96–97, 101, 107, 113, 115, and 119 are from *The Asian Journal of Thomas Merton*, edited by Naomi Burton, Patrick Hart, and James Laughlin (New York: New Directions, 1973), pages 312; 235; 325; 310; 338; 312–313; 233 and 235; and 318–319; respectively. Copyright © 1973 by the Trustees of the Merton Legacy Trust. Reprinted by permission of New Directions Publishing Corp.

The excerpts on pages 30, 74, 79, and 93–94 are from *A Thomas Merton Reader*, edited by Thomas P. McDonnell (Garden City, NY: Image Books, 1974), pages 17, 16–17, 384, and 284, respectively. Used by permission of the publisher.

The excerpts on pages 31 and 63 are from *Contemplative Prayer*, by Thomas Merton (Garden City, NY: Image Books, 1971), pages 29; 30–31 and 30.

The excerpts on pages 31, 32, 42, and 84–85 are from *Contemplation in a World of Action*, by Thomas Merton (Garden City, NY: Image Books, 1973), pages 26, 381, 377, and 172, respectively. Copyright © 1971 by the Trustees of the Merton Legacy Trust. Used by permission of the publisher.

The excerpts on pages 32 and 62 are from *Thomas Merton: Spiritual Master*, edited by Lawrence S. Cunningham (Mahwah, NJ: Paulist Press, 1992), pages 47–48 and 352. Copyright © 1992 by Lawrence S. Cunningham.

The excerpts on pages 34–35, 36, 47, 62–63, 63, 68, 73, 78, 84, 90–91, 96, 97, 98, 99, and 102 are from *New Seeds of Contemplation*, by Thomas Merton (New York: New Directions, 1962), pages 34–36, 7, 127–128, 243 and 217, 235, 32, 296–297, 51, 112, 158, 152, 156, 162, and 64, respectively. Copyright © 1961 by The Abbey of Gethsemani. Reprinted by permission of New Directions Publishing Corp.

The excerpt on page 36 is from "Contemplation," by Walter J. Burghardt (*Church*, Winter 1989), page 15.

Titles in the Companions for the Journey Series

Praying with Anthony of Padua	forthcoming
Praying with Benedict	forthcoming
Praying with Catherine McAuley	
Praying with Catherine of Siena	
Praying with Clare of Assisi	
Praying with Dominic	
Praying with Dorothy Day	
Praying with Elizabeth Seton	
Praying with Francis of Assisi	
Praying with Hildegard of Bingen	
Praying with Ignatius of Loyola	
Praying with John Baptist de La Salle	
Praying with John of the Cross	
Praying with Julian of Norwich	
Praying with Louise de Marillac	
Praying with Teresa of Ávila	
Praying with Thérèse of Lisieux	
Praying with Thomas Merton	
Praying with Vincent de Paul	

Order from your local religious bookstore or from

Saint Mary's Press
702 TERRACE HEIGHTS
WINONA MN 55987-1320
USA
1-800-533-8095